ALWAYS CRASHING

ISSUE TWO

CHICAGO, ILLINOIS • PITTSBURGH, PENNSYLVANIA

Copyright 2019 Always Crashing. All rights to the works published herein remain with the individual authors.

ISBN: 978-0-578-46134-2

Always Crashing is a magazine of fiction, poetry, and nameless things around and in-between. We publish one print issue per year and feature online content year-round. We are headquartered in Chicago, Illinois, and Pittsburgh, Pennsylvania.

Editors: Jessica Berger & James Tadd Adcox

Managing Editor: Helenmary Sheridan

For submission guidelines, ordering information, and access to our electronic edition featuring new work every two weeks, please visit www.alwayscrashing.com

SIDE A

SIDE B

/ side a

FROM *MULTIPLEX*

/ Rebecca Cross

Theater 1 — Matins (First Nocturne)

Lights!

1.
The movie opens as the body opens,

1.a.
with as much trepidation as joy.

1.b.
with stumbling.

1.c.
with light.

2.
In movies, lighting is everything.

The holy trinity: key light, fill light, back light. Sidelights create drama. Kickers make angels. Light can age faces or hide imperfections. Light focuses our attention.

The first movies were light. Light given, withheld. Those magic lanterns projecting goblins and specters onto parlor walls.

Small wonder the first movies were of monsters. There's something otherworldly about bodies on screen.

3.
We watch movies in a night of our own making. Bodies enfolded by red velvet seats. Bodies haloed by the screen's light. Light bending outward, row on row on row.

4.
O blazing canvas! O bloodred curtain!

The bodies onscreen are whitewhitewhite, every flaw erased with
their godportion of light.

Illuminated body! O flatperfect flesh!

5.
The light leaves and enters. The light is a groaning.

The light is alive. O living light! The glow and ah of it.

6.
The screen flickers sympathetically.

It says, *All I am, all you are, is light.*

7.
How do we find ourselves when we are hidden by so much light?

FROM *MULTIPLEX*

/ Rebecca Cross

THEATER 2 — MATINS (SECOND NOCTURNE)

Camera!

THE BODY:
In every body, there is a sadness.

THE CAMERA:
Not least of which is the sadness of watching.

THE BODY:
And being watched.

THE CAMERA:
Naturally.

THE BODY:
Describe yourself.

THE CAMERA:
I am the eye you know best.

THE BODY:
What do you see?

THE CAMERA:
You see it too.

THE BODY:
What do you see?

THE CAMERA:
A body. And beneath that body another. And beneath that
body …

THE BODY:
The camera is the saddest machine.

THE CAMERA:
But I always have a point. A focal point, if you will.

THE BODY:
And what is your purpose?

THE CAMERA:
To see everything. To eat up the light.

THE BODY:
Is that all?

THE CAMERA:
It is everything, being aimed with precision at what I want
to see.

THE BODY:
I admit, I know nothing about cameras.

THE CAMERA:
You know what I show you.

THE BODY:
It's as though you're looking out of my head.

THE CAMERA:
Suddenly, everything is transparent.

THE BODY:
And transcendental. What have you seen?

THE CAMERA:
Enough to want more.

THE BODY:
What will you see?

THE CAMERA:
Everything. It is not for me to demure or abstain.

THE BODY:
It is possible to be too eager to see.

THE CAMERA:
And to be too eager to be mutilated by the eye.

THE BODY:
It can't be helped.

THE CAMERA:
If that were true.

THE BODY:
When you look at me, what do you see?

THE CAMERA:
You have an eye. Why not use it?

THE BODY:
What do you see?

THE CAMERA:
Beautiful knees, just right for begging.

THE BODY:
What do you see?

THE CAMERA:
A script thumbed through.

THE BODY:
What do you see?

THE CAMERA:
The end of all things, I see to the end.

FROM *MULTIPLEX*

/ Rebecca Cross

THEATER 3 — MATINS (THIRD NOCTURNE)

Action!

1.
These bodies are all action and no talk.

2.
These bodies are always on the go.

3.
These bodies are laughing, beautifully, heads thrown back like a dead bird.

4.
These bodies say cute lines like, "Frankly, my dear, this is the beginning of a bumpy ride."

5.
These bodies are trying to find a way out.

6.
These bodies are driving cars recklessly down crowded streets, weaving through traffic, narrowly missing pedestrians, striking street vendors' carts.

7.
These bodies are riding horses across open plains.

8.
These bodies are running after someone on city sidewalks, running away in dark woods.

9.
These bodies are tripping, falling.

10.
These bodies are standing alone in a field of swaying grass during the golden hour.

11.
These bodies are pointing guns at other bodies, holding their guns out like censers, the sacrament of firing a gun.

12.
These bodies are charging through doors, jumping rooftop to rooftop, playing dramatic games of chess.

13.
These bodies are slicing through jungles, rafting down rapids, parachuting out of planes.

14.
These bodies are dancing in unison, all high kicks, pirouettes, splits.

15.
These bodies are demonstrating all the ways in which bodies can show hunger.

16.
These bodies are touched by, touching other bodies.

17.
These bodies lift skirts, unzip pants, unhook bras.

18.
These bodies are rolling together on a beach, waves crashing around them, wet sand sticking to skin.

19.
These bodies are falling in love.

20.

These bodies are reveling in their bodyness.

21.

These bodies have no pimples, foul odors, unwanted hair.

22.

These bodies recognize themselves in other bodies.

23.

These bodies are recognized by other bodies.

24.

These bodies are precious to other bodies.

25.

These bodies are telling us what bodies should be.

THE CAVE

/ Cameron Pierce

And then, like every other night, without fail, I fished a dog from the lake. Gut the mutt heart beating. Skinned and set him over the fire. Ate him up real beastlike. Shit him out a couple hours later. Put the shit-dog in a buggy and set the buggy on fire. The dog was never the same again. Not a dog at all but a human shit in the shape of a skull, spitting shitfire as the buggy careened down the hill into the lake by the sea where I'd originally fished the dog. There was nothing extraordinary about any of this.

My nightly ritual. I, a lonesome, habitual, reclusive earthdweller with no friends and no family, no love for anything and yet hardly a yearning for death. I declined to pray because life left me with few complaints. A rotting tooth, an aching bone, a sad dark hole in the chest where the heart should be. The sky in this time boiled and lurched, gravylike sores oozing noxious gas, peppered by centuries of industrial abuse. The lake by the sea burned the skin if you swam in it, but somehow the dogs remained safe to eat. I'm unsure when dogs became seadwellers.

My responsibility in life is not to know things or proclaim things. I'm neither scientist nor historian. Anyone who expects anything of me is an idiot creep. My endeavors here lie solely in recording the strange occurrence following my nightly dog-eating ritual. After I sent the flaming buggy down the hill and back to the lake, burning bright with dog shit in the polluted night, a ghost came to visit me.

The ghost lurched puppetlike, movements unsure. Initially I mistook the ghost for a wounded human and this frightened me. I had not encountered another human being for months. Then, as the ghost approached, shuffling toward my hovel, I saw that its face was the face of the dead, and relief settled over me. Not that the living dead were all that common, but at least I would not have to fight for my home. I had killed too many to protect what was mine and I did not relish the prospect of killing again. The ghost sat down beside me and looked directly at me and said, "I am you."

"You must be joking," I said.

"Miles from here there is a wishing cave. Inside the cave is the skeleton of a large crustacean, its species now extinct, never known to the human race.”

“How did the crustacean get in the wishing cave?”

“The cave had a wish.”

“And what was its wish?”

“To be the first man on the moon,” said the ghost.

“I’m not sure I follow,” I said, and in truth, I was beginning to grow bored. The ghost’s words, while nonsensical, were no more nonsensical than the world I had lived in ever since the time when things went wrong.

“The cave wished to be the first man on the moon, and the large crustacean, the last of an exceedingly rare species, answered its wish.”

“If this is a riddle, I’m afraid it is beyond me.”

“This is no riddle,” the ghost said. “You see, the crustacean was a psychic and a filmmaker. The crustacean gleaned the cave’s wish from the subatomic matter binding everything in the universe. Touched by the depth of the cave’s desire, the crustacean set about to direct a film portraying the cave on a daring interstellar journey to the moon.”

“Did the crustacean complete the film?”

“Yes, indeed.”

“And yet the crustacean is now dead in the dark of the cave.”

“That is where my story takes a tragic turn. The crustacean, having completed final edits on the film, set out to meet the cave. They had yet to meet in person and the cave had no idea of the crustacean’s existence. During filming, the crustacean spent many nights astrally projecting itself into the vicinity of the cave, but the crustacean wanted their first encounter to be in the flesh, presenting the film to the cave. Several times in the past the crustacean had made introductions in the ethereal space of the mind with others, only for things not to work out when they eventually met face to face.”

“So the crustacean went to see the cave?”

“To show the cave the film depicting its deepest longing.”

“What happened next?” I asked, genuinely intrigued.

“The crustacean was swallowed up by the dark of the cave.”

“What about the film?”

“The film remains inside the cave, clutched tightly in the crustacean’s claw.”

"Did the cave watch the film?"

"That's the irony. The crustacean was a powerful psychic, but not a particularly good one, in part because the crustacean was mentally deranged. The crustacean accurately picked up on someone's desire to be the first man on the moon, but the cave had never contemplated such a thing. Or anything at all. The cave was a thoughtless, normal cave. Except for its all-consuming darkness. The crustacean's efforts were not hopeless, however, because someone else living inside the cave had indeed longed to be the first man on the moon."

"And who was that?"

"That was me."

"So did you recover the film and watch it?"

"I did not."

"But why not?"

"Because I am a ghost and the rule of ghosts is that I am allowed to influence and persuade, but I cannot physically alter anything that belongs to the plane of the living."

The ghost's motive dawned on me. "So you need someone to recover the film from the cave, so that you can watch it."

The ghost's teeth glowed beneath the wretched curl of its smile. "I knew I'd come to the right place. We understand each other so well."

"I hate to break it to you, but there's been lots of people on the moon by now."

"Yes, but not me," said the ghost.

"You can't be the first if someone else has already done it."

"Yes, but I can be the first to be depicted on film as a cave becoming the first man on the moon."

"That would be an extraordinary achievement," I said, entirely believing it, wondering if I'd ever come close to achieving something so incredible.

"So you understand why I must watch the film for myself," the ghost said. "This film could vindicate my entire existence. It could put my restless soul at ease and allow me to pass on to whatever comes after the long night of eternal bullshit I've been living."

I understood. The ghost's story awakened something in me that I had not felt in maybe forever. I felt like I served a purpose beyond eating, shitting, and sleeping. So I agreed to set out the following morning with the ghost, to visit the cave where the large and exceedingly rare crustacean had perished, leaving behind its magnum opus, the film depicting the cave becoming the first man on the moon, where the cave represented the ghost due to shortcomings in the crustacean's incredible yet faulty psychic power.

Lying side by side in the dark of my hovel, surrounded by the wild ugly howling world, the ghost and I were becoming best friends forever.

*

The pink of dawn washed over the dark forest. The night beasts retreated to their hiding places and the creatures of the day emerged, victorious to have survived another night. The colorful dawn was short lived. Pollution clouds rolled in, smudging the sky into marbled streaks of pink and gray.

I ate cold leftover dog while waiting for the ghost to wake. Did the ghost dream? If so, did the ghost dream of its former life, or did it dream of mundane things like I did? I loathed dreaming because dreaming felt like work. I greatly preferred the nights when sleep cocooned me in nothingness. If I ever longed for a god, what I truly longed for was a faceless behemoth with a mouth that swallowed everything. Total erasure. Eventually swallowing the void itself. The fact that I existed at all meant that either my god did not exist or my god had forsaken me. I did not believe that gods tested their followers. Trials and tricks were human contrivances.

Stoking the coals of last night's fire, I set a pot of water for mushroom tea. There was still some meat left on the face of the dog. I picked at the face meat while the water came to a boil. The mushroom tea clarified my thoughts, allowed me to think and see clearly. In a dying world, lucidity meant survival.

The ghost awoke as I sat drinking the mushroom tea. I wanted to ask about its dreams or lack thereof, but the ghost stood abruptly and said, "We must set out for the cave."

I asked for time to drink my tea and pack my hovel, but the ghost strode out into the wasting forest. I had to choose to follow or be left behind. I chugged the tea, scalding my tongue and blistering my throat. And I followed. This was, for whatever reason, a thing I had to do.

"What does it mean to be a ghost?" I asked.

"A ghost is a debtor in the currency of fate."

"I don't believe in fate."

"Then you never have to worry about being a ghost."

"Is belief that powerful?"

"Belief is everything in a make-believe world."

"But surely this carnage," I said, gesturing to the wasteland around us, "is not made up by you and me."

"The theatrical production we call life is dreamed collectively by all participants."

"So why can't we dream of anything better?"

"There's shortcomings in all collaborations."

I was beginning to understand. "You mean we're limited by who and what we are, and that because we're all bound by history, genetics, and our own personal bullshit, we've squandered our rare opportunity to create something beautiful. We're ugly, and we recreate the earth in our own image."

"You learn quickly," the ghost said.

"I take a lot of mushrooms," I said.

This was the furthest I'd ventured from my hovel in longer than I remembered. My daily ritual had remained the same for so long. Wake up, eat cold dog, drink mushroom tea, curl into the fetal position and silently freak out in my mind for the remainder of the day, build a buggy out of sticks, then in the gloaming wander down to the lake, fish out a dog, kill and eat the dog, shit out the dog into the buggy, set the buggy on fire and send it careening down to the lake as an offering, and sleep without dreaming, if I was lucky.

For the past several years, I'd even lost the need to forage for mushrooms. Either due to mass consumption or my negligence in basic hygiene, mushroom cultures took root in the crooks of my body. I harvested the blue, oyster-shaped mushrooms from my armpits and crotch as casually as scratching an itch. They repopulated nightly. Between the dogs and the mushrooms, I'd lost all desire to venture far from my hovel. Now, broken from my routine, I realized the degree of my degeneration. Muscles squandered, skin pale blue, legs more like tentacles with awkward hooves clunking. For so long I'd lived with the deception that even if my mind was gone, at least I remained human in appearance. Walking along with the ghost, I accepted that all humanity had left me long ago.

Uncertainty sustained my outlook as the ghost and I forged a new path through the forest. My skepticism and fear were outweighed only by my unconquerable desire to help. When the ghost reached out for help, it must have sensed a willing victim. And so, shortly after we set out, we encountered a pitiful, starving human on the trail.

"Help me," the human said.

The ghost turned to me and said, "Set this one on fire."

I nodded acquiescently. I lit a match and raised the flame to the tattered shirt of the human. But before I could light the human on fire, I looked into the human's eyes and asked, "Am I human too?"

The human transformed into a gigantic eagle.

"Quick!" the ghost said.

But I was too slow. The eagle clutched the ghost in its talons and carried the ghost high up into the sky. Either as a defense mechanism or due to some biological law governing the living dead, the ghost exploded in the eagle's claws. White leaves, the remains of the ghost, rained down on me. The eagle soared on as though it still clutched its prey. Unable to directly alter physical matter, the ghost had given its life in a diversion tactic in order to save me. At least that's what it seemed. There was no way to know for sure. My spirit guide was gone.

*

Every night throughout my childhood, my father left the house in a different mask. My father, my mother, and I ate dinner at the small oak table pushed into a corner of the kitchen. After dinner, my father drank a cup of coffee. He took his coffee black. I recall no conversations held between my parents during our family dinners, but we were only a family in routine and ritual. Actors, really. I played the role of son. Mother played the role of mother. Father played the role of father. Beneath the charade existed skeletons with black holes for faces. On the outside, good manners and an attention to the details of normalcy hid the silent screams emitting from our gummy mouths. Anyone on the outside could have called our act if only they had seen my father leave the house each night in his masks, but our house was located in a cul-de-sac of a housing tract never finished. The houses surrounding our own lay in stasis—rotting timber and cracked foundations, at best a roof but never any walls. Sometimes I fantasized about living in one of these unfinished houses. Only then, in a house without walls, might some unlikely passerby capture the truth of my father.

One of his few regular acts of fatherly affection occurred after dinner each night, when he finished his coffee, donned his nightly mask, and kissed me on the forehead. Beneath the latex, his breath smelled of milk and tooth decay. I never understood the milkiness of my father's breath. He took his coffee black and we never had dairy products in our house.

Seven nights a week, the masks were different. He had a mask for every day of the week. On Monday, he wore the werewolf mask. On Tuesday, he wore the vampire mask. On Wednesday, he wore the ghoul mask. On Thursday, he wore the extraterrestrial mask. On Friday, he wore the skeleton mask. On Saturday, he wore the ape mask. On Sunday, he wore a mask that was a re-creation of his own face, only much older—and dead. Once, before I knew better, I asked my father where he'd gotten his masks. He looked at me sternly before his eyes softened. "I'm paying off a debt," he said.

Every person carries around their own interior hells. Some are like rooms, or even entire houses. Some people get lost in their hells. Some people invite others inside, trapping them. My father was the minotaur within.

I knew our life was horrible, but until the night my mother died, I never suspected our life to be unusual in any way. We were eating dinner like any other night when her head severed from her neck. The plunk of her head into her bowl of pot roast is a sound I dread to this day.

"You were chewing too fast," my father chided her. "Now look what you've done."

Swiftly, he scooped her head out of the pot roast and carried it off to their bedroom at the end of the hall. I sat quietly at the dinner table across from my mother's headless body, awaiting my father's return. After what seemed like a very long time, he returned from the bedroom in his ghoul mask. "Your mother has taken ill. Clean up after dinner and go straight to bed."

He left the house without drinking his coffee or kissing me on the forehead, but I stuck out my share of the nightly ritual. I finished my pot roast, deferring my eyes from the sight of my mother, and put all of our dishes in the sink when I finished. That night I dreamed of nothing, like every other night. When I awoke, earlier than usual, my father was not yet home. I went into the kitchen and found that my mother's headless body had vanished in the night. In her place a tree had grown. The tree was moss covered and ancient, with thick, pallid leaves that brought to mind the flippers of sea-dwelling mammals. Tiny spiders spun webs among the tree's branches. In an effort to avoid ultimate horror, I ran back to my room and awaited my father's return.

I should have known my father would drag my mother into the backyard and set her on fire. I watched her burn through the grime layer of my bedroom window. To my surprise, my father peeled his ghoul mask from his head. He placed the mask on her burning body like a bouquet of flowers. The mask burbled and bubbled into a plume of black smoke that spiraled out of the backyard and into the marine layer smothering everything. This was the closest my father ever came in my presence—though I doubt he knew I was watching—to showing affection to my mother. I wondered what he would do now on ghoul nights.

I should have probably killed myself at some point or another, but I didn't. Instead I endured in the house with my father. My mother's absence hardly made a dent in our lives. Some days I wondered if she ever existed at all. I may have forgotten about her entirely were it not for the tree corpse in the backyard. Some nights, after my father donned his mask of the evening and left the house, I snuck into the backyard and curled up in the charred remains of my mother and wept.

I'd have never considered following my father on his nightly ritual if it weren't for his sacrifice of the ghoul mask. I perceived my father to be a dangerous animal that I should watch closely but never provoke. That meant I knew his routines and habits, but exclusively for self-preservation. His doings sparked little curiosity. My stunted imagination could not even begin to conceive where he might possibly go each night in his werewolf mask, his vampire mask, or the other masks he wore on a weekly basis. But on the night following the ghoul mask's destruction, my father concluded dinner with his usual coffee, kissed me on the forehead, and left the house sans mask. I'd never seen him do this before. I didn't know what it meant. And for the first time, I felt a strong desire to know more about my father. I needed to know where he went at night. And then one day, the police came. They shot and killed my father. They took me from the home. I was put in a cage in a warehouse full of other cages, each containing a child just like me. They housed us there for months or years, I'll never be certain. One day, a policeman came and unlocked all of our cages. Setting us free, he told each of us, "The world is dying. Nothing is safe. Be careful out there." We children waited until the very last one of us was freed before we turned on the policeman. In our weakened state, we were like jellyfish. However, there were many of us. We overwhelmed him, and we devoured him alive. Then we turned on each other.

*

I found the cave more easily than expected. No epic journey. I crawled inside, consumed by darkness not for the first time. Discovered there the skeleton of the psychic crustacean, clutched in its dead claw the film depicting the cave becoming the first man on the moon. The film cassette fit perfectly into my mouth. Nothing doing. Nothing to do. I coiled snakelike and let the images project from the cassette in my mouth on the wall of the cave. The flickering imagery depicted the cave, in its endless black, flying in a rocket ship to the moon.

The cave was played by a person or creature wearing a dark blanket over its head. The rocket ship was made of sticks and leaves. And the moon was a dead jellyfish, its tentacles cut from its body and discarded, the body of the jellyfish suspended by a rope over an expanse of black sand intended to depict the cosmos. The actor playing the cave descended from the crude rocket ship onto the surface of the jellyfish moon.

Through some trick of perception, the jellyfish moon appeared to be very large, and the cave took several weightless, bounding steps. The film ended shortly thereafter. I removed the cassette from my mouth. Lay in silence. Decided to take up a new occupation. I would be the new ghost of the cave. The psychic crustacean was dead, but if I could somehow resurrect it, it could produce a film of my own wish: I wanted to see where my father went at night, all those years ago. My entire life had been a series of fractured moments and bizarre nightmares. If only I could go back to the start, maybe I could have a chance to be whole again. For now, I curled up in the the husk of the psychic crustacean, in the darkness of the cave. Waiting for the filmmaker to awaken.

MIDSUMMER CROWN

/ Reilly D. Cox

1.

Bot.

When my cue comes, call me, and I will answer.
I have a good speaking voice now, practiced—
can make it any way you want: higher,
lower—hell, my lips are things to be praised.

And I am handsome with my beard, I'm told—
have pretty hair, such pretty, wifely bones,
and were it not for these shoulders! I could fit
any dress (thin boy, flat chest, go home).

But I forget myself! What was my point?
I'm to put on a play, and I am
Hermia, wooed by Demetrius—no,
I am Lysander, wooed by Helena—

Oh, fuck it. We'll skip ahead and be glad:
Methought I was, and methought I had——

Puc. (aside)

Do I wake
    with thee?
Will you mar
    ry me?

or

Gender dysphoria: the condition of feeling
one's emotional and psychological identity
(as male or female) to be opposite to one's
biological sex.

or

a rose is a rose is a rose

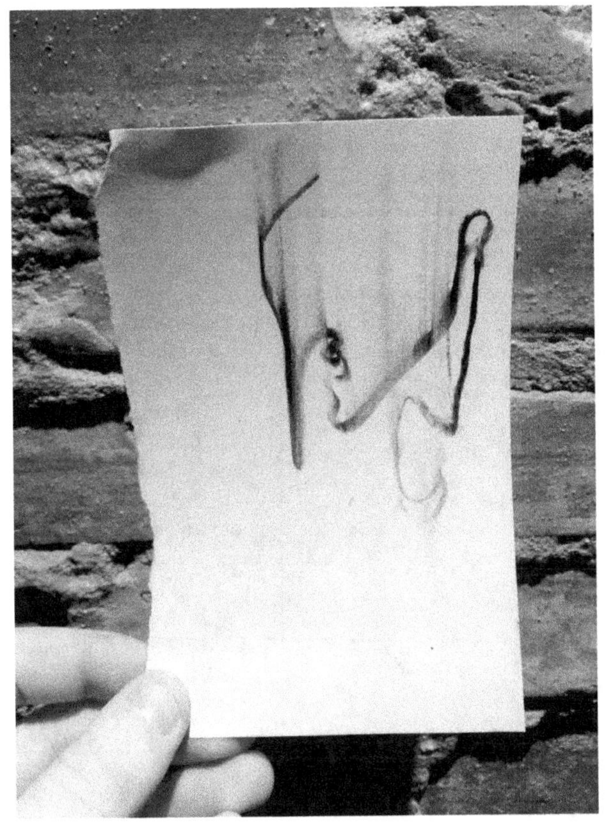

Fig. 1

2.

Fai.

Methought I was, and methought I had
a body. It was the wildest dream!
But no, listen: This new body was clad
in fig leaves, rice—and pure. It was a scream.

No, it wasn't great, young Puck chasing me
around a tree—to call him a rude boy
would be an understatement. But maybe
it was the principle of the whole joy:

strange wood, strange body, strange voice
   (though practiced).
I don't remember most of being young:
the first schoolyard abuse; the first slight kiss.
There was someone nice, but they died, weak
lung:

Either I mistake your shape and making quite,
or else you are that shrewd and knavish sprite—

Puc. (aside)

Do I wake
     with thee?
Will you mar
    ry   me?

Do I wake
     with thee?
Will you mar
    ry   me?

or

Dream interpretation: the process of
assigning meaning to dreams. In many
ancient societies, such as those of Egypt
and Greece, dreaming was considered a
supernatural communication or a means
of divine intervention, whose message
could be interpreted by people with these
associated spiritual powers.

In modern times, various schools of
psychology and neurobiology have offered
theories about the meaning and purpose
of dreams.

or

One perfect rose

Fig. 2

3.

Puc.

Or else you are that shrewd and knavish sprite
who dared to be so rude to his mother
as to ask, *What if I liked boys like I like*
girls? Good Catholic miss, she deserved better.

And father—oh, he was less than happy
when his son came home with purple hair and
    nails.
He was being kind when he said, *When I*
was growing up, only fags dyed their hair.

It was truly for the best: woods and fields
are no place for a fairy. Too many
hunters, too many bright churches. So yield,
put on the long pants, say, *I'm he, he, he.*

And stop dwelling in the past: it's a bore.
Hence, get thee gone, and follow me no more

Puc. (aside)

Do I wake
    with thee?
Will you mar
    ry   me?

Do I wake
    with thee?
Will you mar
    ry   me?

Do I wake
    with thee?
Will you mar
    ry   me?

or

Homophobia encompasses a range of
negative attitudes and feelings toward
homosexuality or people who are identi-
fied or perceived as being lesbian, gay,
bisexual or transgender (LGBT). It has
been defined as contempt, prejudice, aver-
sion, hatred or antipathy, may be based
on irrational fear, and is often related to
religious beliefs.

or

Ash on an old man's sleeve/ Is all the ash the
burnt roses leave.

Fig. 3

4.

Hence, get thee gone, and follow me no more,
said the red hart to the loving hunter.
Do I entice you? do I speak you fair?
But love's made him deaf: he fires closer.

Standing by the edge of the field, I don't
want to be seen, hope that the brown of my
coat blends in with the trees as kisses blown
from a Remington at last catch a thigh

and my heart stumbles. I won't dance again.
Is violence what I get for my rough hands?
I'm deaf in one ear, a liar, but when
the hunter kneels to cradle me, he laments,

I'll follow thee and make a heaven of hell,
To die upon the hand I love so well.

Puc. (aside)

| Do I wake | with thee? |
| Will you mar | ry   me? |

| Do I wake | with thee? |
| Will you mar | ry   me? |

| Do I wake | with thee? |
| Will you mar | ry   me? |

| Do I wake | with thee? |
| Will you mar | ry   me? |

or

The Remington 11-87 is a gas-operated
semiautomatic (autoloading) shotgun, mean-
ing that some of the high-pressure gases
from the burning gunpowder are diverted
through two small holes in the underside of
the barrel. The gases force a piston (and the
bolt) toward the rear of the shotgun, which
in turn ejects the spent shell. A spring then
forces the bolt forward, sending a new shell
from the magazine into the chamber. This gas
operation has the effect of reducing the re-
coil felt by the shooter, since the total recoil
energy is spread out over a longer period
of time than would be the case with fixed
breech shotguns.

or

A rose by any other name would smell as sweet

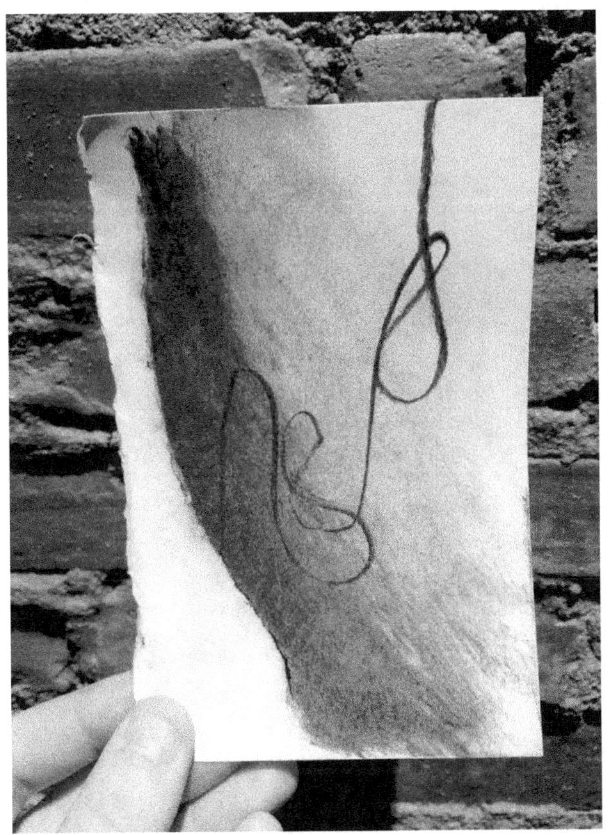

Fig. 4

5.

Lys.   Puc. *(aside*

To die upon the hand I love so well.
Shucking corn. Much a goo about nothing.
Hoisting your own petard. Pocket pinball.
Midsummer night's cream. Straining the main
   vein.

Stay, on thy peril: I alone will go
and what a time I will have! Nervous hands
make good friends and my whole life I've been
   so
nervous. So one might picture a woman,

of all the crazy shit in the world, but
not with anyone else, no—just being,
just having some fucking tea, and somewhat
bored—oh, to be bored and to be reading

Kierkegaard. If my Finite finds me, I'll fuss.
I charge thee, hence, and do not haunt me thus.

Puc. *(aside*

Do I wake   with thee
Will you mar ry   me

Do I wake   with thee
Will you mar ry   me

Do I wake   with thee
Will you mar ry   me

Do I wake   with thee
Will you mar ry   me

Do I wake   with thee
Will you mar ry   me

or

The struggle between the Finite and the Infinite,
   always existing somewhere in between.

or

It is waiting, / like a broken door, like the red dog
that chases its tail and eats your rose- / bushes and
then must be forgiven.

Fig. 5

6.

Dem.

I charge thee, hence, and do not haunt me thus,
and I leave the Athenian sleeping
on the bank of the Styx County creek. Us
men, we belong buried, with our rings

and moustaches and stern looks. Our ashes
might fall *upon a little western flower,*
and cover them, again, but rain washes
away fathers and grandfathers, leaves her

alone to be the good son. She'll be a
bastard some days, will wear dresses to what
funerals allow, and will gather the
sexless flowers for a sexless bouquet:

lilies, mums, narcissus, orchids, and crowns,
Before milk-white, now purple with love's wound.

Puc. (aside)

Do I wake with thee?
Will you mar ry me?

Do I wake with thee?
Will you mar ry me?

Do I wake with thee?
Will you mar ry me?

Do I wake with thee?
Will you mar ry me?

Do I wake with thee?
Will you mar ry me?

Do I wake with thee?
Will you mar ry me?

or

Gynodioecious: having hermaphrodite
flowers and female flowers on separate
plants. Gynoecious: having only female
flowers (the female of a dioecious popula-
tion); producing seed but not pollen.
Gynomonoecious: having both bisexual
and female flowers on the same plant.

or

What was said to the rose that made it open
was said to me here in my chest.

Fig. 6

7.

<table>
<tr><td>

Her.

I dreamed my body was made of love's wounds.
I dreamed my body became a bloom of flowers.

I dreamed I wove my many ghosts a crown
but still was firm, said, *do not haunt me thus.*

I dreamed my hands stopped loving me so well.
I dreamed that I died in this body. Or,

I dreamed I was a deer dressed in small bells,
cursing my tracks, begging, *follow me no more,*

Or, I dreamed I was still a boy, all unclad.
Or else you are that shrewd and knavish sprite

Methought I was, and methought I had
a cup of tea, a boring book, some light.

I'll be Hermia, Puck, or Lysander.
When my cue comes, call me, and I will answer.

</td><td>

Puc. (aside)

Do I wake with thee will you marry me Do I wake with thee will you marry me Do I wake with thee will you marry me Do I wake with thee will you marry me Do I wake with thee will you marry me Do I wake with thee will you marry me Do I wake with thee will you marry me Do I wake with thee will you marry me Do I wake with thee will you marry me Do I wake with thee will you marry me Do I wake with thee will you marry me Do I wake with thee will you marry me Do I wake with thee will you marry me Do I wake with thee will you marry me Do I wake with thee will you marry me Do I wake with thee will you marry me Do I wake with thee will you marry me Do I wake with thee will you marry me Do I wake with thee will you marry me Do I wake with thee will you marry me

</td></tr>
</table>

Fig. 7

notes

1. Overture (with Gender Dysphoria) with a line from Gertrude Stein
2. Sonnet for Fairy (with Dream Theory) with a line from Dorothy Parker
3. Sonnet for Robin (with a laugh) with a line from T.S. Eliot
4. Sonnet for Helena (with shotgun) with a line from William Shakespeare
5. Sonnet for Demetrius (with a line from Siken and Kierkegaard) with a line from Richard Siken
6. Sonnet for Lysander (with eulogy and bouquet) with a line from Jalal al-Din Rumi
7. Epilogue (with Hermia's dream journal)

Illustrations by Brennan E. Cox.

AND THEN SHE SAID…

/ Paulette Beete & Jen Rouse

And then she said if a palm is a ship and the mouth refuses to un-swallow the ocean.

And then she said if I remember everything but the way the sky trembled, the way the ocean sulked, the way no one even tried to walk on water anymore.

And then she said everything can fit in the back corner of the jaw if you remember hard enough.

And then she said if you balance what was said beside what was left on the tongue's underbelly.

And then she said the trouble with the hands is the way they open shut open shut as if mercy doesn't matter.

And then she said what she wanted never to forget was how forgiveness meant the way their words collapsed like waves and met in one mouth.

And then she said the time must come again to be the time now and the time wasn't so much but the way glitter rose from the dust.

And then she said sometimes these two hands must form a vessel. Put your hands in mine.

And then she said this is how the water decides how much it will ever ever love you.

And then she said I am not certain we have met.

And then she said nothing in a whisper.

And then she spoke as one who has come back from a long journey with hands full of water.

And then she said forgiveness was less like a lifeboat and more like a lifeboat.

And then she spoke of all the lies we couldn't agree to drown in the
bucket by the well that was also a lie.

And then she said something that was half joke, half bird.

And then she said these hands are wings and fire.

And then she said desire is an equation, half-broken and half-burned.

And then she said when one adds everything together it equals the
ocean.

And then she said we should return to wings, even if they falter as
though encased in ice.

And then she said I will fly with you, over oceans, and always.

[here the transcription falters and we are left with less than silence]

[here the transcription falters and we are left with the sound of de-
sire bruised into mercy]

SYLVIA PLATH AND HER NEIGHBORS

/ Paulette Beete & Jen Rouse

cento after Sylvia Plath

They're out of the dark's ragbag, these two
tattooing over and over the same blue grievances,
a garden of mouthings. Purple, scarlet-speckled, black.
Suicidal, at one with the drive,

grub-white mulberries redden among leaves
and your first gift is making stone out of everything.
I shall never get you put together entirely
fair chronicler of every foul declension.

Now coldness comes sifting down, layer after layer:
this is the silence of astounded souls.
In this country there is neither measure or balance
and I see myself, flat, ridiculous, a cut-paper shadow.

Once, I was ordinary.
Beyond the interval of now and here,
blameless as daylight, I stood looking.
(Is she dead, is she sleeping?)

Empty, I echo to the least footfall.
For the eyeing of my scars, there is a charge:
You bring me good news from the clinic.
It is you the knives are out for

But I would rather be horizontal
under the eyes of the stars and the moon's rictus.
I'm a riddle in nine syllables.
I do not think the sea will appear at all.

You said you would kill it this morning.
Rubber breasts or a rubber crotch,

I shall never get out of this! There are two of me now:
ghost of a leaf, ghost of a bird.

The abstracts hover like dull angels.
Floating on their delicate feet over the cold pews,
these poems do not live; it's a sad diagnosis
So your gestures flake off—

Over your body the clouds go.

AFTER [FRANCESCO GUARINO'S] *ST. AGATHA*
/ DURING [A BELOVED'S] REHAB

/ Grace O'Connor

she convinces her mother to leave her be,
but receives many proposals—declines.

they sentence her to redlace rooms and
many strange men.

each unstitch their human and re-stitch into
a line of ants scuttling out her door.

they still ask to marry her, and she gives
to her arm muscle.

they bring iron hooks and hot coals and she
watches the pain glow beneath her wrists
and still

they chop off her breasts.

she prays:
there's no better way to see my heart go
than with two holes in my chest.

she holds her breasts
on a gold platter, offers them like loaves.

[Lucy] eats the bread.

and when asked, *what beautiful eyes you have.*
May I have you?

[St. Lucy] unscrews the blues from her head
and offers them.

she arrives: [in a dream]
[fire curled] [valkyrie breath]
laughing, laughing, laughing,
but what did you say?

[sky in my chest heaves open wind]

she watches [me]
[cartoons on a tv] [faces, faces]
three pictures arrive in a message

[the kitchen table splinters]
[flower weight

torture

weight]

but w h a t d i d y o u s a y

[?   ]

have they given

you human

food?

COMA [,]

/ Grace O'Connor

for Briana

When I write a poem about you, I can't
disrobe the earthy weight of where you are[coma—I mean eyelash , bird leg , inter-ruption ,]

and how I'm doing nothing for you except
writing poems. I look at the word: *coma* [I mean breath , or eyelash (again) , oar ,]

It's everywhere, littering my sentences,
especially cluttering my images of you—*coma*[orange peel , finger nail , sliver of skin on the knife-edge ,]

Looks like breath, like stitches, like [the cup's crack , breath (again) , corner rounding , I mean coming , I mean coming to ,]

the cur ve of unused hands.[You can cross and uncross your legs now]

I mean[kome—Greek: hair of the head , the comet's tail , first hair on fire , I mean the first hair a seed releases into the earth , I mean fetal position , I mean born for , I mean against , a steering wheel , or like a worm pulling like sweat through a pore ,]

it looks a lot like a worm pulling
like sweat through a pore[I mean breaking from the deepest sleep]

in the earth.

OVERLAP LAPPING FRAMES SOFT SET RESET ALL S E T, ALIVE

/ Grace O'Connor

NOCTURNE FOR HUMAN DISTURBANCE

/ Grace O'Connor

After Julia Jacobs,"Mammals Go Nocturnal in Bid to Avoid Humans"

I am here.   I am fox.
   I am   split into parts,
two hearts.   I am
   human split in two,
dreaming   for you.
   The dark   —car light
reminds my hair
   to ignite.   I have
an extra   digit on each paw.
   This does not help me run.
My human brain   is a car light.
   There is a light at the end
of my retina.   I

   cannot reach it.

There is   a tree
   with no gravity, leaking   birds.
They go upward.   I

   cannot reach them.

I am crawling   because I am
   a fox on fire.

There is a ladder   decaying
   in a rut, jut   up,
a lost clavicle.
   & when I touch   it
with my paw, it   turns
   limp thread & fire.

Then,   instead,

a house.
   and in the house   they
are happy.

I am interruption, am human.

   They   are happy
in the light of a small, glass sun.
   They   have a tee shirt and
chest and they   touch   their breasts.
   Beneath, cardiac &   alive.

I   am interruption, am fire.

   And I   am happy   they
are happy.
   And   I am happy   they are happy to touch
their skin   above cardiac   warmth.

I am   without   hands.
   My fox clavicles point north,
but here   north is up and I cannot.

I peel a layer from my best heart to offer.
   I am told it is not   enough
to cover anything.   Not now.

   What is the size of a fox heart, anyway?

What and which surface area may I cover or keep?

   I   can't go any faster,
and my four extra claws
   slow me down.

There is no room in my undone heart,
   but I am lighter now.

I am interruption,   am heart.

I climb from   the ground
    into the dreamdark.
I am a stray running   over a road.

    There is no traction now.

I float into the sky's retina.

    The mourning doves cleave through a maple,

their wings singing a startling frequency.

I   do not return.

CARDIOVASCULAR COLLAPSE

/ Shane Jesse Christmass

Interlock in the street. They're flung from limp flints. Burning scents. Eyesores. Coloured parts of the sky. Green leaves that drift in the tide of the East River. Embankments of knotted grass. I glance back at the East River. A wire fence. Communication with other open beings. Idle machines. A short walk to the bathroom. She's doused in blonde mechanisms. A torn genus of deadly moth. The wife lurking in the good values of degeneracy. She tears Juan Carlos's clothes off… actions recorded in unpublished histogram. Unfamiliar people are irritating. GIF GIF GIF GIF. Juan Carlos lays flat. The dying art of breath. Arturo disappears under his wife's cotton dress. This nightmare of a giant man… his red mouth moves… disposing of him… let alone murdering him. Juan Carlos stares madly at Arturo's wife. Downtown in the South end of the city… a mist-hung gun whips up the mob. BWAP BWAP. Arturo sobs in the pale dawn. Someone else screams. The strange assignment of lace doused over Arturo's wife. Dinner chairs burning in a Pizza Hut car park. Juan Carlos opens the window… calling out swiftly to his interior voice. This skin draped over burn victims to restore sensation. Hands tied behind my back. Optic implants. Certain times of the year the city gas lamps have their supply cut off. Bionic limbs. Artificial organs on sale at Bemelmans Bar. Arturo sweeping out the sickroom. The door ajar. A well dressed… rather wise looking man hanging around the murder scene. Private prisons dot the landscape. Potatoes and mash and gloom for prisoners. People leisurely walk down to the East Village. Juan Carlos stands up… unsteadily panting. Arturo ushers him onto the gangplank grinning. POTUS on the television screens. Juan Carlos ushers everyone out onto the terrace. He presents a paper on the human-machine symbiosis. He's into it. A millionaire who wants to live forever. He will make it happen. Augmented reality. Too much government interference Juan Carlos notes. Cashmere jackets with MIDI controller interfaces. A special line of credit. Rat protection. This is the part where you admit that you talk about me. That's the idea. The idea rings true. I have an alias for every hotel in Battambang. I'm quite happy with the new idea. A couple of questions before I join Arturo in bed. The woman's voice is urgent. I brood… order drip coffee… croissants. I have my own ideas about my education. Men as thieves. Indefinable thievery. An undernote creeps in from the dusty sidewalk. Remodelled machines… tanks and armoured cars. Bookshelves with bomb plans. Evidence coming in from the crosswire. Suitable result: murder. Arturo's delicately chiselled lips mean I've always been alone here… sick in Battambang drawing the rats. Photographing them too. Khmer folks who work in barber shops and laundries hitting up their friends… spying on them… selling them out… pushing them down wide stairs… taking their year of profits… giving it to the police. An old man in the assembly room. He crawls over the inch-thick carpets… his ignorance very defective. Four guys fondling each other around the outhouses. Money in my pocket. My driver backs the car up… silence now. Someone to share my joy. The police have an authority to give fingers. Juan Carlos is back from the jungle. He mumbles something about his violent temper. Bloodthirsty reputation. There's no evidence in my manuals to suggest this. Wives along the marketplace. Hungry… unclothed children. Rifles and cartridges… perpetual debris… elements of warfare. No explanation needed. Arturo comes into the apartment with a surly… stiff-haired dog on a leash. There are strays everywhere in NYC now. Night settles over the East River. Arturo lights a candle. Our only form of illumination. No dictionaries on the shelf. Her shoulder draped in cloth. She repeats certain phrases. Her slender features still in check. I possess decidedly… as she disrobes. Arturo pours dishwashing detergent and motor oil on the carpet. The usual squalid side streets. Arturo will be safer here than anywhere. Trouble in the hallway. Pistols drawn from under the bedsheets. Confusion above all things. Impossibly amused and satisfied. The hallway is full of cab drivers. They snort into their pails. I'm pushed to the brink. Juan Carlos dishes out orders. Pushes his silly ideas against shooting accidents. Drinks at four. Money. Polluted lobsters with identification bracelets around Arturo's brow. Constantly unfolding elements… Juan Carlos notices the disgust. Arturo presses demands onto Juan Carlos. Chemical leaching understood through haptic perception. Priestess Psychic nose on her. Bruises. Trains in the rail yard pull out. Blood drained from Arturo's boss. No needs for faces in NYC. Spit cloth around shoes at Grand Central Station. Unsound chairs. Mouldy reeds. He rolls spindly cigarettes between his fingers. Juan Carlos is at the water's edge. Foliage in the East River. Swamp. Oily carnage polluting. Horizon stumbles. Body swelters. Livers and lungs washing ashore in Astoria. Indefinite lifespan in Juan Carlos's sweat having a bath using the restroom sinks. Jehovah's Witnesses with clipboards. Post-humans jammed up the front of the Staten Island Ferry. Cryo-patients chipped and thawed by jackhammers and drills. I turn to Arturo. A smirk. Insects nestle in my ear. Rubbish pecked by the overpass it floats under. Brambles of body. Breath huffed over peeling lips. Inside the Gramercy Park Hotel. Exploding bombs outgrow modern effete civilization. Robotic self-replication… molecular manufacturing. They're building the O'Neil cylinder out in Morristown. Trance-like on Ward's Island. The homeless buried out on Potter's Field/Hart Island. Supercomputers plugging out of gene therapy. Perpetual studying and reexamining of infrawaves under the East River. We upend ourselves. We leave. Sullen stroll. Breeze of twilight. Stars pull in sombre darkness. East River pours into drain. Water against concrete… splashing… running below the overpass. Water amongst plastic bags… ash sticks… Styrofoam. Night is an airless step. Juan Carlos suffocates. Office blocks. Arturo and I down by the East River. Arturo is open thoughts and feelings. I have no money left. This isn't my place. Sit down… have a drink. That's warm stuff… that's warm drink stirring inside. The posing… the pushing of the crowd. Alejandra pulls out a bottle of Seroquel. We eat bowls of awful winter season. . A meatpacker in NOHO warehouse mass-producing medical modifications that permanently alter or replace the excretive function of the human body. An ugly scene. Daft prototypes. Arturo promoting involuntary cochlear implants. Ears removed at birth replaced with headphones/transistor earpieces. Uptown Manhattan now has more citizens whose bodies contain prosthetics. Birth-hands sheared off and exchanged with cybernetic ones. Robotic exoskeletons rejected by war veterans as being unfashionable. The handicapped would rather crawl. Juan Carlos wearing high-tech surgical gloves. Weekday. Juan Carlos makes small-scale models of the United States. Vacuum gauges under hot sweat. Air pressure overhead. He is alone. Old cigarette packets. He cuts his artery using a pair of shears. Suits/well-known brand name. Billboard advertising. Television documentaries that outline the beauty of jelly... Savagery of the human contribution. The rubbish bin on clear cold mornings. Windless afternoons. Arturo dips four fingers into an orange juice. A girl stands aside as Juan Carlos enters the room. He shuts me out. Wax effigy. Arturo turns the music off. She's got a molten centre. Juan Carlos blots out mechanisms. Torn residue caused by GIF melting. Genus of deadly moth. Arturo splices the mainframe with good values of a dead community. The dating website holds degenerates. Arturo tears Juan Carlos's clothes off. He has a decorative outline. Half-deliberate actions recorded in unpublished histogram. Unfamiliar cocaine deals with those who believe people are irritating. GIF profiles on dating websites. Laughing fits. Language of GIF. Reports from police designed to intimidate us... Juan Carlos is glad Arturo has made this sacrifice. He's mad to resist her charms. Unpleasant news from the newspapers. A package of money. Eyebrows twitch. The house cleaner is here. She's craving excitement. I tell her to get in the swimming pool then the hot tub. There's a mix-up in this prosthetic business. Simple villages being burnt to the ground. The customary low roof aflame. Free women on fire. A horrible mess. She had eyes only two days before. Arturo watches... then marches inside. A large picture frame. She hangs onto one of the balustrades. The rats come in with a driver waits for me. Four patients... five nurses. My secretary fills out the medical forms. The doctor extracts scorched piece of metal from my back. An extra meeting is called because of the delay at the hospital. Arturo lies next to me... hoping I will get better... padding the wound with a rolled-up sock. I'm downloading Kampuchea as a country onto my laptop. This country is unknown to electrical faults. My eyelids rub the offending eye. Bullet casings at the bottom of this file. The phone rings. We have some trouble. Reports coming in from Laos. Juan Carlos tells me how he escaped from NYC. A medium-sized cigarette in his hand. I want the full picture. A cursing man pulls out into the street. He has a little portable stand where he sells American groceries to Englishmen. There's nothing actually scientific about it. Strangers sheltered and remaining in shadows. The morning sunshine. Tobacco in the pocket of my coat. I little expected it. I disliked it. War victims... the bandaged ones all line the street corners. Some are prettier than others. Inspection of our papers... identification... what's in our boots? Another flood. Soldier as silent as a traffic cop. The man behind the counter nods. I go off to the sick room. Me in Battambang. Flat-out no chance. I walk uptown past the modest little apartments. I take a seat at the food place behind the cleaning-and-dyeing plant. Tables and garment racks weed the sidewalk. Juan Carlos saunters along and takes a seat. I'm reading the appointment schedule in my notebook. No new television shows to watch. Our temples crack. Emotions are a belt notch. Inside the hotel… Juan Carlos logs onto dating websites. Description as infantile attempt. Laughing fits and Pepsi-Cola on the laptop screen. Juan Carlos is staggered. He has no idea how to describe himself. He's all at sea. Would marriage be beneath him? Something like that. Does he excuse himself from the table once he finishes corn soup? That sort of thing. Image assistants uploading glamour shots of themselves. Juan Carlos describing his time on the planet. How Several minutes later… sweat forms on Juan Carlos doesn't know much. Juan Carlos doesn't stay on the internet very long. GIF cleaned smoothly… systematically. Alejandra's cornea. I poke and fork it out. My cornea makes headlines. Miley Cyrus takes the naked trend too far with nipple pasties for a top. I torch the newspaper. He tried to slide… then penetrate in my body. Sea and space colonies on the subway barbequing commuter's faces. Buskers all bored. Juan Carlos standing in the driveway… lit up by the streetlights. Juan Carlos holds his weapon and fires plant spores. Gas bottles under the chairs. I open my suitcase. Stacks of bundled underwear inside. Alejandra smirks in drunken style. Damp… cheap words fall from her mouth. Just don't get lonely. A group of children with their parents. Alejandra leans in from her chair. She wears a T-shirt. I'm visible in the dark. I take my last breath. The shadow of anorexics. It's Monday. On the ground. He completes his work inside the company's holiday villa. He reads the instruction manual several times. There is more than one narrative in the instruction manual. Juan Carlos works besides vacuum gauges under hot sweat steam and pressure overhead. He is alone— once more—working. Track suits/brand name. Billboard's advertising TV documentaries that outline the beauty and savagery of the human contribution. The process of strengthening and integrating CPU into plastic brain moulds. Arturo slides into midnight. Crimson-stained. Emotional signs include sighs and deep breaths. The door opens. Take that. Pincers. GIF living in an upstairs place containing a soft drink dispenser… a coffee table… a double bed in the corner... a refrigerator filled with foodstuffs and amphetamines. GIF as wax effigy/molten centre. Juan Carlos blots out the elemental residue caused by GIF melting. Arturo splices the mainframe with a dead community. The dating website now has a decorative outline. Half-deliberate cocaine deals with those who believe in dating websites. Laughing fits. Language with a small moustache and keen eyes. Juan Carlos Tribes of Amazonians. Bloodied hearts on electroshock cables. Juan Carlos writes on a Post-it note... his cursive in unique form. Juan Carlos goes to his job. 3 p.m. on a weekday. Juan Carlos makes clumsily fashioned small-scale models of the United States. Juan Carlos takes a swig of synthetic water. Wife wields her hips over Arturo. The dawn on a projection screen. Nothing brings my attention to it. The sun rises. Xerox of a Xerox over Manhattan. Bubbling fat on Juan Carlos's skin. Bright lights... loud music... young kids. Arturo's wife is a cardboard cut-out. She's in the doorway. She turns the music Vermouth in a trough. Television light projectiles in the night. Vibrant against Juan Carlos's skin. Some talk about nurses. Juan Carlos lays flat on the packing crate. Product placements on NBC. Arturo walking leisurely down to the East Village. Holograms of Lindsay Lohan's autopsy. Pipettes of poisonous bacteria and Dilaterol. Syrup... tables and injections to assist in mind-uploading to the internet. Juan Carlos's senses in a heightened way. Enhancements to fingertips that make the electrical properties of tissue more profound. Juan Carlos conducting targeted ultrasounds on reclaimed cult members. In Washington heads roll off into the East River. Head rubber-rolls off like doll's head. Bloodied hair lock in the sewer. Flesh that smells like bromine. Arturo throws a leg bone into oncoming traffic. Juan Carlos turfs outdoor chairs. Free cigarettes drop from zeppelins over the Manhattan skyline. Food packages burning in the Bronx. People who want to remember. Arturo drinks a vanilla milkshake. I fall silent and look around in surprise. We make it out to Atlantic City. The seaside stay agrees. Huge pacifiers blowing out from Washington Bridge. CPU into plastic brain moulds. Further famine. Juan Carlos slides into midnight. Crimson-stained. Emotionally employed like this. Traffic signs include sighs and deep breaths. A contingency of assistants opening the door. The red mouth of Arturo moves. Voice disposes with marvellous intellect. War veterans murder Juan Carlos. Dark complexions. It's a fine day and Juan Carlos stares at Arturo. The sun sparkles. Juan Carlos logs onto dating websites. A mist-hung sun over NYC. Description as infantile attempt. Laughing fits whip up the mob. Pepsi-Cola on the laptop screen. Arturo sobs. Juan Carlos staggers. He has no dawn. Someone else screams. The strange idea of how to describe himself. The sun rises. Xerox machines. GIF as wax effigy. A Post-it note at the company's holiday villa. Juan Carlos reads the note. The cursive is a unique form. Juan Carlos reads the instruction manual several times. Juan Carlos goes to work. 3 p.m. on a Coal barges up the East River. A grey colour… massive skyline. Deforestation in upstate NY. Rope binds around Juan Carlos's wrists. Drinking at the Starbucks up on Columbus Avenue. Pharmaceuticals. The emotions of humans as animals. Arturo winds her hair right off at the roots. Food fights. Arturo catches my eye. She's rawboned… sharp-cornered and skinny. Effects in sand dunes protect from spilt oil. I'm going out in the November midmorning. Febrile bodies… high-arching bones… heavy diarrhoea on the doorstep of the Goodwill store on W 72nd Street. Similar processes. Ticket stubs. Bottles of brandy. Moist cocaine. Can't move it at all. Hand reconstruction. Recluse and CIA detainee. I'm going to Netflix all the yellow cabs on the isle of Manhattan… search for universal payoffs… prerogatives and the object of contract between two beings on the shorelines of the East River. I give my appointment schedule another glance… another reading. Horse-drawn carts disappear into the stable. Too many people to bribe… however their wives like opening up to the imbecile type. I might be in luck. Trick things… like booby traps and hand grenades in my apartment. A knock on my door. Arturo just checking in to see if I'm home safely. Paranoia. I'm on the second floor. They couldn't see me from the street. Infrared not working on their gadgets. I place myself into Arturo's mouth. It's open with blood draining onto my doormat. Welcome. I ask him where the best place to get a bus timetable is. Bus terminal. Bus station. Bus stop. It's morning. Newspapers to be collected. Several articles have been authorised without my knowledge. One catches my eye… something about trying to get a vineyard industry up and going. Truck impact over the back of the bus seat. A giant weather balloon… I am not sure. The size of the hot dog is normal… all unsorted gravel material… all lacklustre. Arturo looks both ways. I'm going to head into the subway… breathe out the frosting air… and light a cigarette. Accumulating stock and bond investments. Taking out a massive health insurance policy. Economy in a slow but steadily increasing decline. Inflation at 24%. A beheading in Times Square… during the intermission of *The Lion King*. Shuttle busses from CUNY for people to watch. Rubber at the sculpture. The nose is missing. She attaches the nose. Arturo hurries to the elevators. A squeak catches her attention. She looks across the station… nothing but a homeless person on the bus. A packet of sugar on the dresser. Parcels of meat wrapped in butcher's paper going mouldy. Arturo hunches over… snatches down a size. This toxic condition is more than our bones. I enclose you. I'm going to photocopy your face at funerals. This is the result… a radiation of bony fish… crab mains and ballooning ocean… the factors which affect geometry. Reports on the war dead aren't reported. First Republic Bank shuttering Steinway & Sons Piano Factory. Juan Carlos is confused. NYC is the pawn of a unilateral power. Arturo was born in Kentucky. Arturo was born in Kentucky. He moved itinerantly before settling in Oakland. Temperatures rise… so does the suicide rate. It is pushing out to 300… 000 to 400… 000 monthly. Half of that is failed attempts… those that end up hospitalised. Bombings over the mountain ranges. The 'Hollywood' sign. I lift a petty cash box onto my half-eaten sandwich. Sawn abdomens hidden in haversack. I strip down to my underwear. A marionette copy… all blushed cheeked. A voice over a loudspeaker in the background. Myself on a bus heading up 9th Avenue. Sea water dribbles into the subway. Narrow bodies. Abandoned snakes. Counterfeit handbags on Canal Street. We go to sleep. Shot clocks buzz on the basketball court. Prosthetics twitch on the shoulder of the expressway. Tears roll down Arturo's face. Robots act as unusual animals. Native cats sleep inside Port Authority Bus Terminal. News ticker splutters in deflated pixels. Further silence. Children dope smoking for ISIS. Police in civilian clothing advance with mace rifles… squinting in the sunlight… pulling at the rope with a noose at the end. Netflix offers a season's pass for advertisements. Replacement hips. Tobacco… one extract. Cocaine again in the bathroom. Faces gleaming through the Manhattan haze. My fingers down the sinews of Alejandra's body. One old man altogether on bench in Washington Square. He turns to his daughter's books… her fashion magazines all tangled. He picks up a piece of wood… inspecting it. Daughter's hair the shade of the icy background. Her money purse rolling down Broadway like tumbleweed. Juan Carlos can't be bothered. Juan Carlos looks at the statue of the child. Jetsam falls away from a dead man. The jungle floor. GIFs rendered as sentences backed with marvellous intellect. Girls as women… dark complexions. It's a fine day and the sun is sparkling. She walks to the table. Rubbish piled up outside. I drink water from the garden hose. I eat strawberries. He constructs models using old cigarette packets. He cuts the packets using a pair of shears. He balances the models on rivers of jelly… configuring shy damsels from the rubbish bin… on clear cold windless afternoons (if you're interested). Translated famine. Juan Carlos never thought he'd be employed like this. He never thought he'd have a contingency of assistants helping him. He sees caterpillars turning into crows. Pesticides. Stomach withdraws further. Bracelet rusting on Alejandra's arm. Sandbags whips my head. Daybreak. Alejandra dresses in white limbs. Petrol cap in her hand. Here you go she mentions. A man behind her. I'll never be able to match her. She's annoying. She asks me over to oversee her operations. Foldout chair inside the front door. I draw back breath. Cement vaporising. The wood of the front door splinters. Clouds of dust and fireworks. Tanks in Times Square fishtailing taking giant shots of brandy. Fire in the hearth. Someone Sideways. Soldiers stomping heads halfway between BB King Blues Club & Grill and the MTV Studios. Coffee shop for lease. Retail shop for lease. Single shot. His head disappears entirely. A torrent of blasts rips into the burning house. Bricks destroyed. Twice I hear Alejandra mention she is the way they painted the hallway. A red-haired old timer opens a new packet of cigarettes. I've run out. No accord with her hostility. Disciplinary action taken against Alejandra. I'm in the same room as her. I'm lost in this. Alejandra looks outside. Someone is spying on her. I run to the windowsill. Demolition time. My future. Cubicle closed by shower door. Soap in the shape of opals. Soap taste inside mouth. Dogs pat sex dolls. Hair locks. Arturo hikes up the hill. War veterans annoy me with deck chairs. Index fingers snap in two. Offal in a bucket. Rib cages churn in serrated gristle. Hard drives made of membrane. The amount of war is absurd. A rock on the carpet. The corridor. It fills with secretaries. Arturo heads over to the payphone and picks up the receiver. A warm summer afternoon. The meat flesh is mislaid… overlooked. A widower with his shirt wide open. Buttons pop everywhere. Arturo and Juan Carlos laugh anyway. Transplants and antibodies set off in cargo holds for Northern Africa. I look over my shoulder. Nothing behind me. I have a spare key. I guess I could stay at the hotel. Arturo looks over the original notes from the autopsy. JPMorgan Chase forecloses on 23 mortgages in Morningside Heights. A middle-aged woman looks at me. She ices her voice. Look at her! She's up. Running. Peeling off into tide. Into her room. The woman looks old. Metallic typefaces on subway entrances. Woman runs forward. Outlandish motion. Fidgets. Twitches. Get me out of here. A bread roll spins on the hotel stairs. Drawstrings undone on my pyjamas. Arturo picks my pyjamas up off the floor. An ambulance crashes out on FDR Drive. Ground coffee in his small moustache. His two legs broken. Body in a wheelchair. The stars come out every third night in Manhattan. Our arrival @ JFK in the winter of 1017 far out over the death lands. Police siren wailing. The paper strainer making wallpaper again. Fingers spread out limply. Sheets of blank paper. I walk the corridor. Taking spare change from the alms box. The crowd at Times Square… Penn Station falls back into the subway. Fleeing with ravenous eyes and muttering mono-syllabic. Humped all the way from the Hudson River up 42nd Street… past the Actors Studio into the bar of the Algonquin Hotel. Ushered and sat into booth for a late lunch of hamburger and hash browns and draught beer. Waiter tear up our order. Ring-modulated voice lies beneath sunken faces. Too louche to be religious.

~~KAWAGAKI~~ DISEASE WAS WAFTING ~~FROM JAPAN TO CHINA~~

/ Dave Brennan

1

My phone lit with the Facebook page of a spree killer.

The neighbors' decapitated heads set on their doorstep in order of age: father, mother, son, daughter, daughter.

Heads anonymous in their otherness.

2

In 1944, *Life* magazine posted this Picture of the Week: a perky American girl penning a thank-you note to her boyfriend for the Japanese skull that lay on the table beside her.

Animal electricity conducted through a metal spike driven out the top of the skull.

Following her boyfriend's death in the Pacific theatre, for the next half-century the girl displayed the skull prominently in her home, inviting all her guests to explore its phenomenal electrical proper-ties.

The politest of her guests, upon touching the rod breaching the skull, would startle, as if jolted by shock.

Most thought her daft.

Following her death in 2005, the skull was sold to the website re-alshrunkenheads.com, from which it was purchased by a business-man in Shanghai.

His bizarre misuse of the skull will be noted only for its joviality.

3

Contagion dizzy with the want of body.

Left to ponder its condition, took to the airwaves, a riddle astride a bullet, a trollop astride a bugger, carving ricochet in the winds over the Sea of Japan.

Born of the clod thwarting the hole, monetarily self-conceived, confusing the execution of the gawker with the culpability of the voyeur, spectacle with the exploitative.

Drug-resistant oddment thrown to the airwaves, formaldehyde oceanography, interlude imaginable only as desolation, as engine, an overlap of video and stills depicting the murder of the search, nascent hum.

The shores of China grew close. Beddable contagion, translator of this violent book,

I captured the moment you first sexed a body to sweet obliteration.

It was the most popular video on the Internet, until it wasn't.

~~IN CHINA, A~~ PIGLET ~~WITH A PENIS ON ITS~~ ~~HEAD WAS~~ REJECTED BY ITS MOTHER

/ Dave Brennan

This night in his crown.

This dark prayer transpired.

When the mind, unbidden, speaks its own spent horn.

When the groin, bare and smooth, simulcasts this abandonment.

Sackless worm—

That he may propagate by headbutt.

That his art, transposed, wakens.

Like a bedsheet rinsed of sleep.

Like a dawn skirted in floral print found bit to death, and risen.

Let it go, mother, let go the waggle.

Where his mind rises, give your rump.

Where the womb rinses itself of dreams and ghosts, there is your home.

~~RESEARCHERS CORRELATED ACTIVA~~
~~TION OF THE DOPAMINERGIC SYSTEM~~
~~IN THE MEDIAL ORBITOFRONTAL AND~~
~~MEDIAL PREFRONTAL CORTICES WITH~~
~~THE PASSIONATE STAGE OF~~ ROMANTIC
LOVE, ~~ACTIVATION OF THE POSTERIOR~~
~~CINGULATE CORTEX WITH THE SENSE~~
~~OF HAVING A BODY, ACTIVATION OF THE~~
~~INSULA WITH CERTAINTY ABOUT THE~~
~~TRUTH OF A NONTESTABLE PROPOS~~
~~TION, AND EXCEPTIONAL ACTIVATION~~
~~OF THE PRESUPPLEMENTARY MOTOR~~
~~AREA AND THE MIDCINGULATE CORTEX~~
WITH ~~THE EXTEMPORIZING OF~~ BRITISH
COMEDIANS

/ Dave Brennan

British buffoonery like jazzy jismings

Acerbic soliloquies sung by the luminous ass

Needy neophytes nudely necking

Libel, the brain's favorite fuckbuddy,
laughs like a cow lapping the Ganges

Yip! Yah! Yahoo! Yooha!

Nor self knows naught of nobody

~~STRANGE FACE ILLUSIONS APPEAR~~ ~~WHEN~~ TWO STRANGERS ~~ARE ASKED TO~~ GAZE AT ~~EACH OTHER IN~~ THE DARK

/ Dave Brennan

1
Dead's the breast, blind and crooked.

Dead is flesh skeletons skittled between high school lockers.

Dead's the walking dead reduced to tilling gardens.

Dead is memory box hanging from a gallows.

Dead's the small, cold room where you learned to unlove yourself.

Dead is a consequence of teeth.

Dead's a cut-up scavenged from the skull.

Dead is animal primped for autopsy stitch.

Dead's a financial condition inherited from the air-conditioned.

Dead is the sex mound, pickled, resurrected.

Dead's a way of death.

2
I want to tell you a story, but I'm no storyteller.

Then tell me the story you don't know, the one of the geraniums on the family plot.

I dressed them and I fed them, until they fell to fragments, their bones rolled to dust by the wind. Ashes scattered atop a grave, a dying piled atop a dying, the new

American way of death.

Recomposed of our disfigurement.

Recomposed of our rootlessness.

The soil pulverized.

There are better ways to tell this story. There are armies slipping
through the night carrying photographs of caved-in heads. Their
own heads. That is not the story, or even a secret. Armies disperse
and take their dead with them. The dead stay behind and take up
the lives of the living.

Dead's the bones that stayed put.

TENNIS PLAYERS' GRUNTS ~~RISE IN PITCH DURING THE MATCHES THEY LOSE~~

/ Dave Brennan

Whether for aesthetic, moral, religious, political, social, scientific, or any other reasons,

too many young tennis players feel that they have do what other tennis players are doing and to believe as they do.

Assumptions about tennis and about the role of the grunt may be perceived by the tennis player as *intuition*. They may become conscious of what they have absorbed from their cultural environment. They may choose other ways of grunting than those they've received without fully realizing it.

I should mention that tennis is often sung.

Sometimes thousands of people come to hear and cheer on the most cherished grunters of the country, indeed, of the world.

This back and forth creates an immensely seductive tension.

Of course, if the resolution is anticlimactic, the audience may well respond with boos.

In post-match conversations, audience members consistently mention how much they savor the grunt, more than almost any other sound. They also talk a lot about the sensuous play of grunt over volley, and whether grunts coincide with pauses in play or cut against them.

Some tennis players attempt to enliven their grunts with active trills and fresh gutturals. Some feel a more regularized rhythm with recurrent stress patterns better evokes the tone and feeling of the experience. The contrast in tone and movement is instructive, as it becomes easier to isolate a failed grunt to hold up and admire for its ineffectiveness.

Many players feel that grunting across volleys is a highly intellectual, even abstract undertaking. Players weren't always grunters. One must master the rules of a particular grunt like the steps of a dance or the form of a poem.

The point is to try to keep the volley pushing ahead and draped across the end-lines in variable ways by employing the correct grunt.

A grunt should occur at intervals regular enough as to suggest method, with a consistently regular timbre, and should become part of the match's music. By the end of the match, there should be some surprising release from these formal expectations. The use of irregular grunts helps to keep the mind focused on intuitive motion rather than lapse into pause. That is, to destructively sift the moment for meaning.

Some players say that a match without grunts is like playing with the net down.

The net being all forms of punctuation and inflection.

Some players, those less inclined toward song, consider their grunts jagged descriptions of a purposeful and ongoing encounter with physics. Physics a cooperative and disenthralling form of worship.

The grunt emphasizes an attentive consciousness.

To grunt without sound, as any player will tell you, marks a breach of faith. In the game. In the song.

A gruntless player is but a whisper, a whisp. Misserved. Lost.

~~DOCTORS ANALYZED THE~~ COMPULSIVE ~~JOKING OF A FIFTY-SEVEN-YEAR-OLD~~ ~~CALIFORNIA MAN WHO PRESENTED~~ ~~WITH A~~ TENDENCY ~~TO HOARD COFFEE~~ ~~GRINDERS AND HAWAIIAN SHIRTS AND~~ TO DEFRAGMENT ~~HIS CO-WORKERS'~~ ~~HARD DRIVES WITHOUT THEIR PERMIS-~~ ~~SION~~

/ Dave Brennan

The real world is enormous and I kept getting skinnier, an inconceivably skinny ghost

-writer whose mouth spewed strange things: a roller coaster, blacksmithing tools, bombardier beetles.

I took life drawing classes at night, to better formulate an objection to the biology of existence, and before you object, let me point out, as a defender of the assembled, I am not the insane taxidermist you would paint me as;

my interest in detail but a reflex to my quibble with how closely I could hew to the ineffability of the physical.

Perhaps we only care how much we resemble the literature of myths.

At home I built a box inside which I could sit and sew a quilt adorned with profiles of the beasts that sprung from my weakly body: dementia, stronger bones, better sex, tenderly vengeful food fantasies.

Two quilts emerged, both the blank shade of green tea, both thin like cheap clothes. I lay beneath them in a swamp of drool.

I grew so skinny I walked only on tiptoe. I buried the bookmark I'd fallen in love with, her death warped the more by the children she'd born us,

a set of twins with so much sunlight

between them that all the creatures of the world were illuminated
in that interval, every actual creature bookended by the supernor-
mal avarice of our nurslings, whose likenesses

I drew and drew until I could no longer deny my findings:

Babies are the original monsters.

/ side b

OF ADDER AND APE

/ Gregg Williard

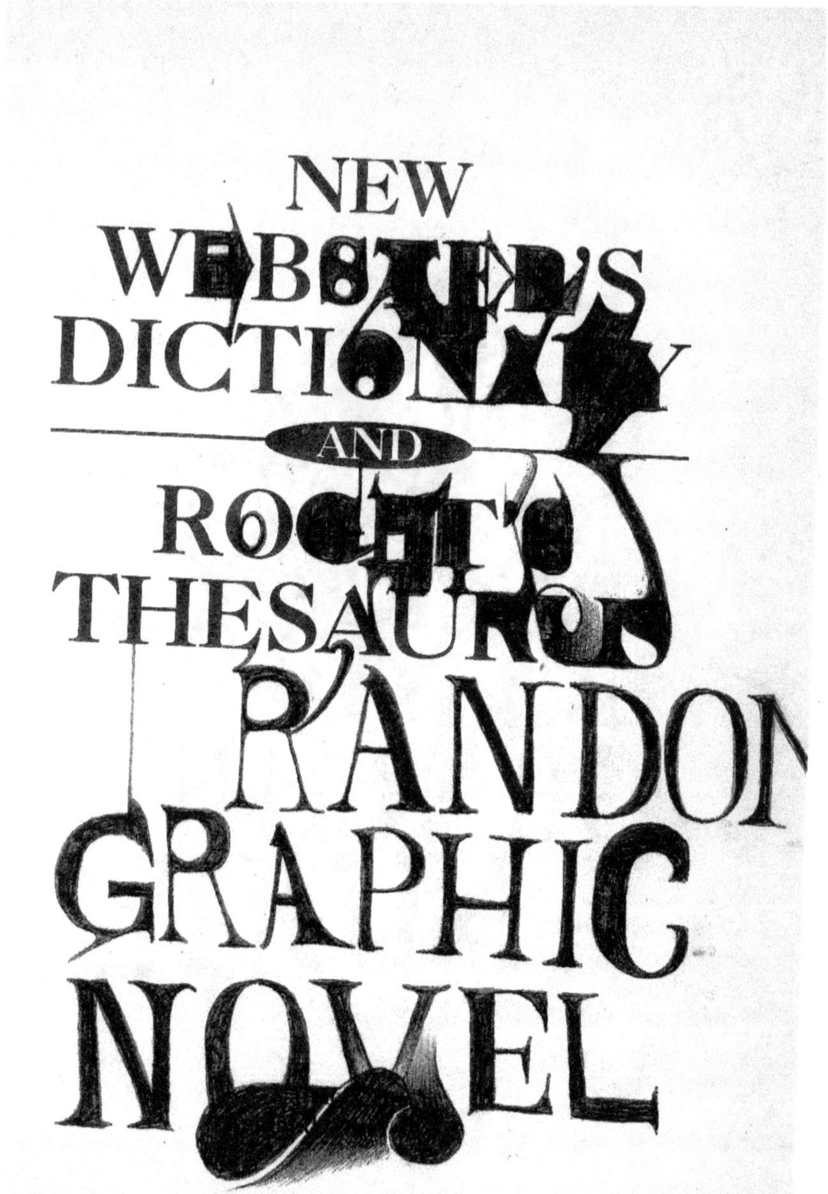

NEW
WEBSTER'S
DICTIONARY
AND
ROGET'S
THESAURUS
RANDOM
GRAPHIC
NOVEL

CONTENTS

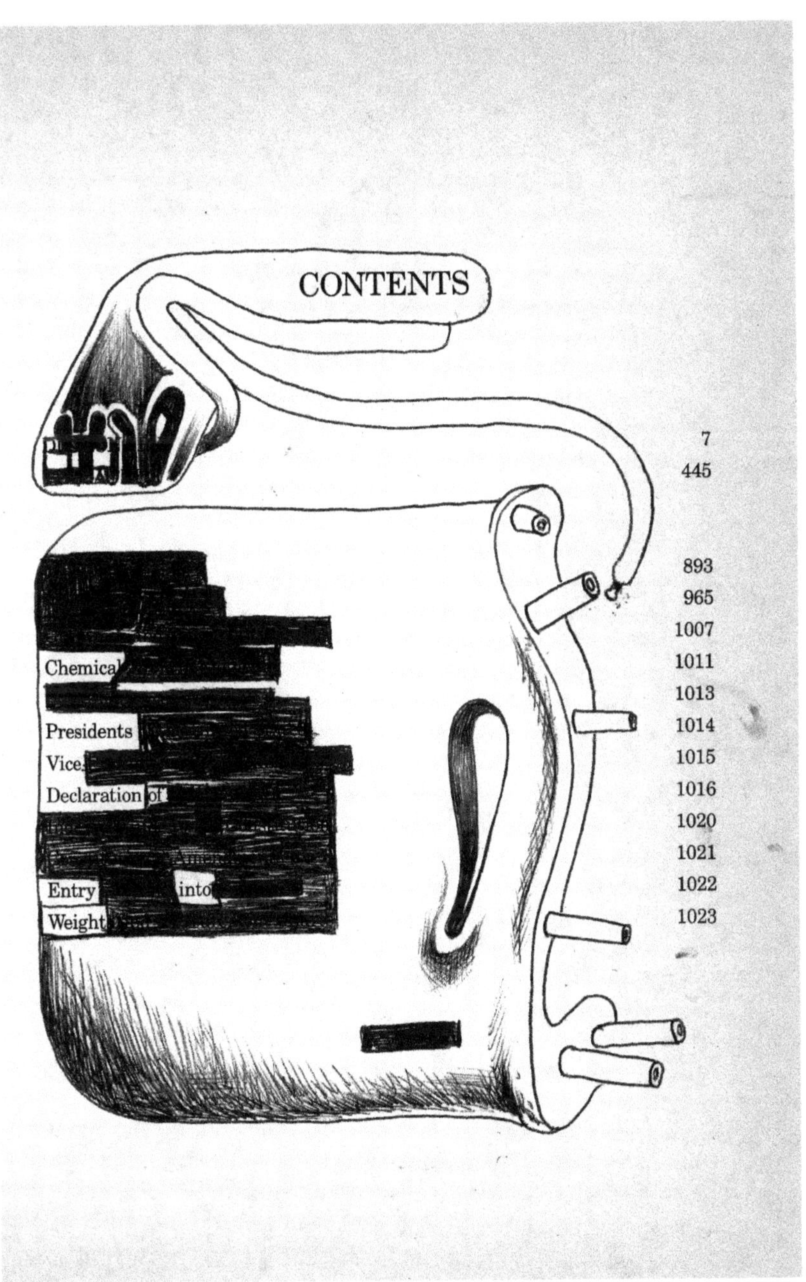

CONTENTS
Chemical
Presidents
Vice
Declaration of
Entry into
Weight
7
445
893
965
1007
1011
1013
1014
1015
1016
1020
1021
1022
1023

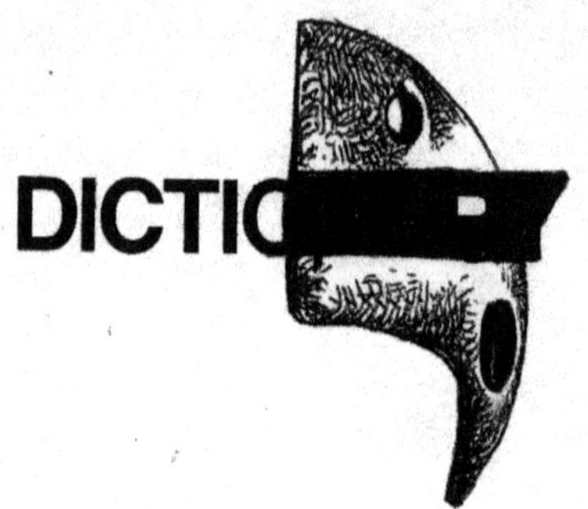

DICTIONARY

OPERATIONS AND PERAMETERS:

- ONLY BALLPOINT PENS

- ONLY RANDOM OPERATIONS i.e.
  (POINT WITH EYES CLOSED,
  OR USE NUMBER OR LETTER
  SYSTEMS BASED ON WHATEVER,
  TO SELECT WORDS THAT WILL
  GUIDE THE NOVEL).

KEY TO THIS DICTIONARY

The entries in this Dictionary are arranged in groups, derived and related words being placed under the main entry.

A. Each main entry, in bold-face type, is syllabified, with the phonetic spelling and accented syllable shown in parentheses. The part of speech, in italics, follows; then the definition.
Ex.: **cross** (kraws) *a.* intersecting; interchanged.

B. Subentries are shown in bold-face type following the definition of the main entry.

1. If a hyphen precedes the subentry, the ending (or the word) is added to the main entry.
Ex.: **-ing** (read **crossing**)
2. If a dash precedes the subentry, a hyphenated word is indicated.
Ex.: **—examination** (read **cross-examination**)
3. If a dash and a space precede the subentry, the words form a spaced compound expression.
Ex.: **— reference** (read **cross reference**)

C. The etymology of the main entry is found in brackets following the entry paragraph.

Note: Irregularities of verb forms, plurals and comparisons are included as sub-entries to facilitate word usage.

PRONUNCIATION GUIDE

These pronunciation symbols are used for the sounds indicated by the bold face letter or letters in the key words.

Vowels and diphthongs:

		Consonants:	
a—bat	ī—bite	b—bill	ngg—finger
ȧ—botany	ō—boat	ch—church	p—pill
a̧—about, soda	oo—book	d—dill	r—rill
(unstressed)	ö̈—boot	f—fill	s—sill
ā—bait	oi—boil	g—get	sh—shall, sure
aw—bought	ou—bout	h—hill	t—till
e—bet	u—but	hw—wheel	th—thin
ē—beet	û—butte	j—judge	TH—then
i—bit	ur—Bert (stressed)	k—kill	v—villa
i·—city (final syllable)	er—blubber (unstressed)	l—lily	w—will
		m—mill	y—yet
		n—nil	z—zillion
		ng—sing	zh—pleasure

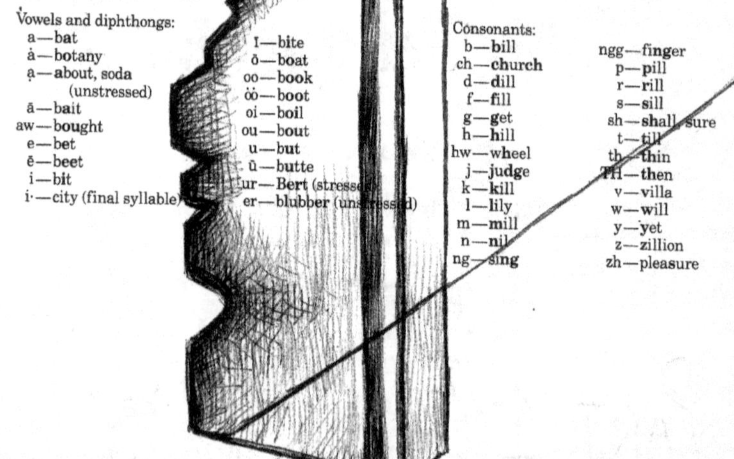

ABBREVIATIONS USED IN THIS DICTIONARY

a. adjective
abbrev abbreviation
ablat. ablative; ablatival
Aborig. Aboriginal
acc. accusative
A.D. Anno Domini
(in the year of Our Lord)
adv adverb
Aero. Aeronautics
Afr. Africa; African
Agric. Agriculture
Alg. Algebra
alt. alternative
Amer. America; American
Anat. Anatomy
Anglo-Ind. Anglo-Indian
Anthropol. Anthropology
Ar. Arabic
Arch. Archaic
Archaeol. Archaeology
Archit. Architecture
Arith. Arithmetic
Astrol. Astrology
Astron. Astronomy
aux. auxiliary
Aviat. Aviation

Bacter. Bacteriology
B.C. before Christ
Bib. Biblical
Biol. Biology
Bot. Botany
Br., Brit. British
Braz. Brazilian
Bret. Breton
Build. Building

c. about (L. = *Circa*)
C. Centigrade; Central
Can. Canada; Canadian
Cap. capital letter
Carib. Caribbean
Carp. Carpentry
Celt. Celtic
cent. century
Cent. Central
cf. compare (L. = *confer*)
ch. Chapter
Chem. Chemistry
Chin. Chinese
Class. Myth. Classical Mythology
Colloq. Colloquial; Colloquialism
Comm. Commerce; Commercial
comp. comparative
conj. conjunction
conn. connected
contr. contraction
corrupt. corruption

Dan. Danish
dat. dative
def. art. definite article
demons. demonstrative
der. derivation; derived
Dial. Dialect; Dialectal
Dict. Dictionary
dim. diminutive
Dut. Dutch
Dyn. Dynamics

E. East; English
Eccl. Ecclesiastical
e.g. for example (L. *exemplia gratia*)
E.Ind. East Indian
Elect. Electricity
Embryol. Embryology
Engin. Engineering
Entom. Entomology
Ethnol. Ethnology
Etym. Etymology
Fahr. Fahrenheit
fem. feminine
fig. figuratively
Finn. Finnish
Flem. Flemish
Fort. Fortification
Fr. French
freq. frequentative

Gael. Gaelic
gen. genitive
Geog. Geography
Geol. Geology
Geom. Geometry
Ger. German
Gk. Greek
Gk. Myth. Greek Mythology
Gram. Grammar

Heb. Hebrew
Her. Heraldry
Hind. Hindustani
Hist. History
Hort. Horticulture
Hung. Hungarian

Icel. Icelandic
i.e. that is (L. = *id est*)
imit. imitation; imitative
imper. imperative
impers. impersonal
Ind. Indian
indef. art. indefinite article
indic. indicative
infin. infinitive
interj. interjection
interrog. interrogative
Ir. Irish
It. Italian

Jap. Japanese

L. Latin
l.c. lower case letter
L.Ger. Low German
lit. literally
Lit. Literature
L.L. Low (Late) Latin

masc. masculine
Math. Mathematics
M.E. Middle English
Mech. Mechanics
Med. Medicine
Metal. Metallurgy
Meteor. Meteorology
Mex. Mexican

M.H.Ger. Middle High German
Mil. Military
Min. Mineralogy
Mod. Modern
Mus. Music
Myth. Mythology

n. noun
N. North; Norse
Nat.Hist. Natural History
Naut. Nautical
neg. negative
neut. neuter
nom. nominative
Norw. Norwegian
n.pl. noun plural
n.sing. noun singular
N.T. New Testament

obj. object; objective
obs. obsolete
O.E. Old English
O.Fr. Old French
O.H.Ger. Old High German
O.L.Ger. Old Low German
O.N. Old Norse
Onomat. Onomatopoeic
opp. opposite; opposed
Opt. Optics
Ornith. Ornithology
O.T. Old Testament

Paint. Painting
pa.p. past participle
pass. passive
pa.t. past tense
Path. Pathology
perh. perhaps
Pers. Persian
Phar. Pharmacy
Philol. Philology
Philos. Philosophy
Phon. Phonetics
Photog. Photography
Phys. Physics
Physiol. Physiology
pl. plural
Poet. Poetry; poetical
Pol. Polish
Port. Portuguese
poss. possessive
pref. prefix
prep. preposition
pres. present
Print. Printing
prob. probably
pron. pronoun
Pros. Prosody
Prov Provincial
pr.p. present participle
Psych. psychology

q.v. which see (L. = *quod vide*)

R. River
R.C. Roman Catholic

recip. reciprocal
redup. reduplication
ref. reference; referring
refl. reflexive
rel. related; relative
Rhet. Rhetoric
Rom. Roman
Rom.Myth. Roman Mythology
Russ. Russian

S. South
S.Afr. South African
S.Amer. South American
Sans. Sanskrit
Scand. Scandinavian
Scot. Scots; Scottish
Sculp. Sculpture
sing. singular
Singh. Singhalese
Slav. Slavonic
Sp. Spanish
St. Saint
superl. superlative
Surg. Surgery
Sw. Swedish
Syn. Synonym

t. transitive
Teleg. Telegraphy
Teut. Teutonic
Theat. Theatre
Theol. Theology
Trig. Trigonometry
Turk. Turkish

U.S.A.) United States (of America)
usu. usually

v verb
var. variant; variation
vi. verb intransitive
vt. verb transitive
vulg. vulgar

W. Welsh; West

Yid. Yiddish

Zool. Zoology

PART 1: "Josephus and the Ablution-Adder"

Josephus, WAS
An abbot, doing ablutions in the dark one
night, discovered that

WHEN HE   A

the candle on the table

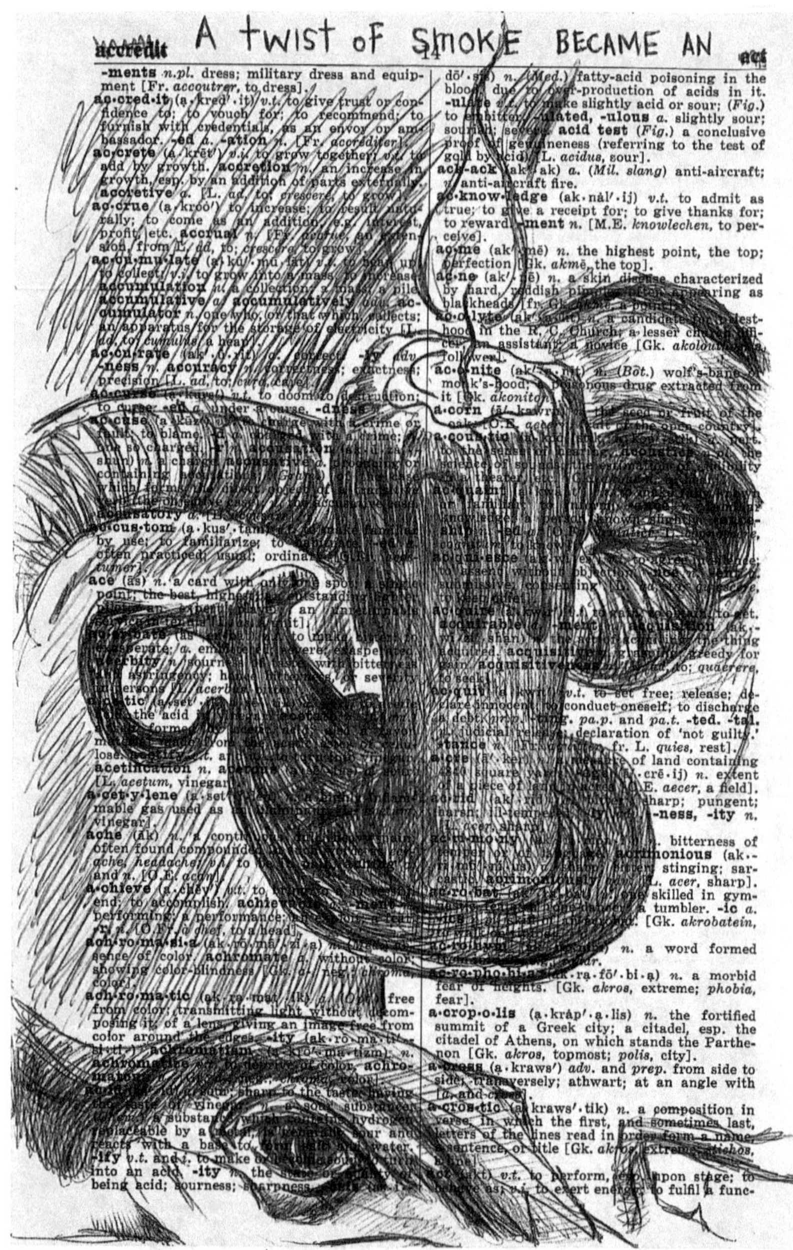

A twist of SMOKE BECAME AN

tion; to operate. *n.* deed; performance; actuality; action; a decree, law, edict, or judgment; principal division of a play. **-ing** *a.* performing a duty; performing on the stage; serving for, as *Acting Captain.* **-or** *n.* one who performs. **-ress** *n.* a female actor [L. *agere, actum,* to do].

ACTH Adreno-corticotropic-hormone used in the treatment of rheumatic diseases.

ac·tin·i·a (ak·tin′·i·a) *n.* the sea anemone. *pl.* **actiniae** [Gk. *aktis,* a ray].

ac·tin·ism (ak′·ti·nizm) *n.* the radiation of light or heat; the property possessed by the sun's ray, of producing chemical changes, as in photography. **actinic** *a.* pert. to actinism. **actiniform** *a.* having a ray-like structure [Gk. *aktis,* a ray].

ac·tin·i·um (ak·tin′·i·um) *n.* a radio-active element; symbol **Ac** [Gk. *aktis,* a ray].

ac·ti·nol·o·gy (ak·ti·nál′·a·ji·) *n.* that branch of science concerned with chemical action of light [Gk. *aktis,* a ray; *logos,* word].

ac·ti·no·ther·a·py (ak·tin·a·ther′·a·pi·) *n.* the treatment of disease by natural or artificial light rays; often known as 'sunlight treatment' [Gk. *aktis,* a ray; *therapeia,* service].

ac·tion (ak′·shan) *n.* a thing done; behavior; physical movement; function; battle; the development of events in a drama, etc.; legal proceedings; (Chem.) effect. **-able** *a.* affording grounds for legal proceedings.

reflex action, an involuntary response to a sensory impulse.

ac·ti·vate (ak′·ti·vat) *v.t.* to make active. **activation** *n.*

ac·tive (ak′·tiv) *a.* having the power to act; agile; busy; alert. **-ly** *adv.* **activism** *n.* policy of those who seek activation. **activist** *n.* one who advocates activism. **activism. activity** *n.* [L. *actum,* to do].

ac·tu·al (ak′·choo·al) *a.* existing now or as fact; real; effective. **-ity** *n.* reality. **-ize** *v.t.* to make actual. **actualization** *n.* **-ly** *adv.* [L. *actus,* a driving].

ac·tu·a·ry (ak′·choo·a·ri) *n.* a registrar; clerk; an official of an insurance company. **actuarial** *a.* **actuarially** *adv.* [L. *actuarius,* a clerk].

ac·tu·ate (ak′·choo·at) *v.t.* to put into action; to incite; to motivate. **actuation** *n.* **actuator** *n.* [L. *actus,* a driving].

a·cu·men (a·kū′·men) *n.* quickness of perception or discernment; sharpness. **acuminate** *a.* pointed.

a·cute (a·kūt′) *a.* sharp-pointed; sharp, subtle, penetrating; (Med.) of disease, with severe symptoms and sharp crisis; (Geom.) less than a right angle. **-ly** *adv.* **-ness** *n.* **acute accent,** a mark (′) over a letter, as in French, to indicate pronunciation [L. *acus,* a needle].

ad *n.* (Colloq.) advertisement.

A.D. (*an·no Dominī*) in the year of our Lord [L. *anno Domini*].

ad·age (ad′·ij) *n.* a saying or maxim that has obtained credit by long use; a proverb; a byword [Fr. *adage,* fr. L. *adagium,* a proverb].

a·da·gio (a·da′·ji·o) *a.* & *adv.* (Mus.) slowly; expressively; a slow movement, in a symphony or sonata. **adagio cantabile,** slowly, in a singing manner [It.].

ad·a·mant (ad′·a·mant) *n.* a stone of impenetrable hardness; the diamond; *a.* very hard; unyielding. **adamantine** (a·da·man′·tin) *a.* [Gk. *a-,* neg.; *damaein,* subdue].

Ad·am's ap·ple (ad′·amz a′·pl) *n.* projection of cartilage at the front of one's throat.

a·dapt (a·dapt′) *v.t.* to make fit or suitable; to make to correspond. **-ability, -ableness** *n.* the quality of being adaptable. **-able** *a.* that may be adapted; versatile. **-ation** *n.* the gradual process of adjustment to new physical conditions exhibited by living organisms. **-er** *n.* any appliance which makes possible a union of two different parts of an apparatus. **-ive** *a.* **-ively** *adv.* **-iveness** *n.* **-or** *n.* a device to make possible the use of a machine, tool, etc. with modification [L. *ad,* to; *aptare,* to fit].

add (ad) *v.t.* to join, unite to form one sum or whole; to annex; to increase; to say further. **-able, -ible** *a.* **-er** *n.* a machine which adds; a comptometer. **-ibility** *n.* **-ition** *n.* the act of adding; anything added; the branch of arithmetic which deals with adding. **-itional** *a.* supplementary; extra. **-itionally** *adv.* **-itive** *a.* to be added; of the nature of an addition [L. *ad,* to; *dare,* to give].

-ad·dend (ad′·end) *n.* number to be added.

ad·den·dum (a·den′·dam) *n.* a thing to be added; an appendix. *pl.* **addenda** [L.].

ad·der (ad′·er) *n.* a venomous serpent [M.E. *an addere* for *a naddere,* fr. O.E. *naeddre,* snake].

ad·dict (a·dikt′) *v.t.* to apply habitually; habituate. **addict** (ad′·ikt) *n.* one addicted to evil habit, e.g. drug-taking. **-ed** *a.* devoted, wholly given over to. **-ion, -ness,** *n.* [L. *addicere,* to assign].

ad·dle (ad′·l) *v.t.* to corrupt; putrify; confuse; to muddle. **addle, addled,** *a.* diseased, rotten; putrid; unfruitful. **-brained, -headed, -pated** *a.* confused [O.E. *adela,* filth].

ad·dress (a·dres′) *v.t.* to direct in writing, as a letter; to apply oneself to; to make a speech; to present a congratulatory message or petition; *n.* a formal speech; manner of speaking; direction of a letter; skill. **-es** *n.pl.* attentions in courtship. **-ee** *n.* person to whom a communication is sent. **addressograph** *n.* a machine for addressing envelopes, etc. [Fr. *adresser*].

ad·duce (a·dūs′) *v.t.* to bring forward as proof; to cite; to quote. **-nt** *a.* or *n.* **adducible** *a.* **adduction** *n.* **adductive** *a.* drawing together; (Anat.) **adductive** *a.* tending to bring towards. **adductor** *n.* adjacent muscle [L. *ad,* to; *ducere,* to lead].

ad·e·no- (ad′·e·no) prefix a combining form. **-itis** *n.* inflammation of the lymphatic glands. **-oid** *a.* of a glandular gland-shaped. **-oids** *n.pl.* swelling of tissue between nose and throat [Gk. *aden,* gland].

a·dept (a·dept′) *a.* thoroughly skilled in any art; an expert; a proficient; an expert [L. *adeptus,* having attained].

ad·e·quate (ad′·e·kwit) *a.* equal to; sufficient. **adequacy** *n.* **-ly** *adv.* [L. *adaequatus,* made equal].

ad·here (ad·hēr′) *v.i.* to stick fast; to be devoted to; to be of the same opinion). **-nce** *n.* state of adhering; steady attachment. **-nt** *a.* united with; or to; *n.* a supporter of person or cause. **adhesion** *n.* act of adhering. **adhesive** *a.* sticky; tenacious; *n.* an agent which sticks things together. **adhesively** *adv.* **adhesiveness** *n.* [L. *ad,* to; *haerere,* to stick].

ad·hib·it (ad·hib′·it) *v.t.* to use or apply; to attach [L. *adhibitus,* added to].

a·dieu (a·dū′) *interj.* good-bye; farewell; *n.* a farewell; a leave-taking. *pl.* **adieus, adieux** (a·dūz′) [Fr. meaning, "to God"].

ad in·fi·ni·tum (ad in·fa·nī′·tam) to infinity, without limit [L.].

ad in·ter·im (ad in′·ter·im) in the meantime [L.].

a·di·os (a·dōs′) good-bye [Sp.].

ad·i·pose (ad′·i·pōs) *a.* pert. to animal fat; fatty. **adiposity** (ad·i·pás′·i·ti·) *n.* fatness. **adipic** *a.* pert. to, or derived from, fatty substances [L. *adeps,* soft fat].

ad·it (ad′·it) *n.* horizontal or inclined entrance into a mine [L. *aditus,* an entrance].

ad·ja·cent (a·jā′·sant) *a.* lying close to; adjoining, bordering on. **-ly** *adv.* **adjacency** *n.* [L. *ad*, to; *jacere*, to lie].

ad·jec·tive (ad'·jik·tiv) *n.* a word used with a noun to qualify, limit, or define it; *a.* pert. to an adjective. **adjectival** (ad·jik·tī'·v'l) *a.* **adjectivally** *adv.* [L. *adjicere*, to add].

ad·join (a·join') *v.t.* to join or unite to; to be next or contiguous to; *v.i.* to be next to. **-ing** *a.* [L. *adjungere*, to join to].

ad·journ (a·jurn') *v.t.* to put off to another day; to postpone. **-ment** *n.* [L. *diurnus*, daily].

ad·judge (a·juj') *v.t.* to settle judicially; to pronounce judgment; to award; to regard or deem. **adjudgment** *n.* **adjudicate** (a·jōō'·di·kāt) *v.t.* to settle judicially; *v.i.* to pronounce judgment. **adjudication** *n.* **adjudicator** *n.* a judge [L. *adjudicare*, to award as a judge].

ad·junct (ad'·jungkt) *n.* something joined to another thing, but not essential to it; (*Gram.*) a word or phrase added to modify meaning; *a.* added to; united with. **-ive, -ively** *adv.* [L. *adjunctus*, united to].

ad·jure (ad·jōōr') *v.t.* to charge or bind, under oath; to entreat earnestly. **adjuration** *n.* a solemn command on oath; an earnest appeal. **adjuratory** *a.* [L. *adjurare*, to confirm by oath].

ad·just (a·just') *v.t.* to adapt; to put in working order; to accommodate. **-able** *a.* **-ment** *n.* **-er**, **-or** *n.* arrangement; settlement; adaptation [L. *ad*; *justus*, just].

ad·ju·tant (aj'·a·tant) *n.* an assistant; staff officer who helps the commanding officer issue orders. **adjutancy** *n.* the office of an adjutant. **adjutant bird** *n.* species of Indian stork [L. *ad*; *juvare*, to help].

ad·lib (ad·lib') *v.i.* and *v.t.* to improvise something; to speak impromptu. *ad libitum* at pleasure [L.].

ad·min·is·ter (ad·min'·is·ter) *v.t.* to manage; public affairs; to govern; to dispense, as justice or punishment; *v.i.* to apply, as a remedy; (*Law*) to settle the estate of one who has died intestate; *v.i.* to give aid. **administrable** *a.* **administrant** *a.* executive; *n.* one who administers. **administration** *n.* the executive part of a government; dispensation; direction. **administrative** *a.* **administrator** *n.* (*fem.* **administratrix**) one who directs; executor of any kind [L. *ad*, to; *ministrare*, to minister].

ad·mi·ral (ad'·mi·ral) *n.* a naval officer of the highest rank (graded as—admiral, vice-admiral, rear-admiral). **-ty** *n.* rank or authority of an admiral; maritime law [Fr. *amiral*; Ar. *amir-al-bahr*, prince of the sea].

ad·mi·ral (ad'·mi·ral) *n.* a species of butterfly, esp. the red admiral.

ad·mire (ad·mīr') *v.t.* to regard with wonder and approval; to esteem, or affection; to prize highly; *v.i.* to wonder; to marvel. **-r** *n.* **admiring** *a.* **admiringly** *adv.* **admirable** *a.* **mi·ra·ble** *a.* excellent; worthy. **admirably** *adv.* **admiration** *n.* wonder mingled with esteem, love, or veneration [L. *ad*, to; *mirari*, to wonder].

ad·mis·si·ble (ad·mis'·i·bl) *a.* allowable; **missibly** *adv.* **admissibility** *n.* **admission** *n.* permission to enter; the price paid for this [L. (part. *admissus*, allowed to go].

ad·mit (ad·mit') *v.t.* to grant entrance; to concede as true; to acknowledge. *pr.p.* **-ting.** *pa.p.* and *pa.t.* **-ted. -tance** *n.* permission to enter [L. *ad*, to; *mittere*, to send].

ad·mix (ad·miks') *v.t.* to mingle with something else. **-ture** *n.* [L. *admiscere*, to mix].

ad·mon·ish (ad·mān'·ish) *v.t.* to reprove gently; to instruct or direct. **-er** *n.* **admonition** (ad·ma·ni'·shan) *n.* rebuke. **admonitory** *a.* [L. *ad*, to; *monere*, *monitum*, to warn].

ad nau·se·am (ad naw'·shi·am, also naw'·zi) to a sickening degree [L.].

a·do (a·dōō') *n.* fuss; bustle; trouble.

a·do·be (a·dō'·bi·) *n.* sun-dried brick [Sp.].

ad·o·les·cence (ad·a·les'·ens) *n.* stage between childhood and manhood; youth. **adolescent** *a.* growing up; *n.* a young man or woman [L. *adolescere*, to grow up].

a·dopt (a·dapt') *v.t.* to receive the child of another and treat it as one's own; to select and accept as one's own, e.g. a view. **-er** *n.* **-able** *a.* **-ion** *n.* **-ive** *a.* that adopts or is adopted [L. *ad*, to; *optare*, to choose].

a·dore (a·dōr') *v.t.* to worship; to love deeply; **-r** *n.* a lover. **adorable** *a.* **adorably** *adv.* **adorableness** *n.* **adoration** (ad·a·rā'·shan) *n.* profound veneration; ardent devotion [L. *ad*, to; *orare*, to pray].

a·dorn (a·dawrn') *v.t.* to decorate; to deck or ornament; to set off to advantage. **-ing** *a.* beautifying; ornamental. **-ment** *n.* ornament; embellishment [L. *ad*, to; *ornare*, to deck].

ad·re·nal (ad·rē'·nal) *n.* a small, ductless gland situated close to upper end of each kidney (same as *supra-renal*). **adrenalin** (ad·ren'·al·in) *n.* the hormone of the adrenal glands; the most effective hemostatic agent known [L. *ad*, to; *renes*, kidneys].

a·drift (a·drift') *adv.* and *a.* floating at random; at mercy of the wind and tide; (*Fig.*) at a loss.

a·droit (a·droit') *a.* dexterous; skillful; ingenious. **-ly** *adv.* **-ness** *n.* [Fr.].

ad·sorb (ad·sorb') *v.t.* aid of solids, to condense and hold on the surface. **adsorption** *n.* [L. *ad*; *sorbere*, to drink in].

ad·u·late (ad'·ū·lāt) *v.t.* to praise or flatter in servile way. **adulation** *n.* **adulatory** (aj·a·la-) *a.* [L. *adulari*, to flatter].

a·dult (a·dult') *a.* grown to maturity, or to full size and strength; appropriate for a grown-up; *n.* a grown-up person. **-ness** *n.* **-hood** *n.* [L. *adultus*].

a·dul·ter·ate (a·dul'·ter·āt) *v.t.* to debase by addition of inferior material; to vitiate; to corrupt; *a.* guilty of adultery. **adulteration** *n.* act of debasing a substance [L. *adulterare*, to defile].

a·dul·ter·y (a·dul'·ter·i·) *n.* violation of the marriage vows. **adulterer** *n.* (*fem.* **adulteress**). **adulterous** *a.* pert. to or guilty of adultery. **adulterously** *adv.* [L. *adulterare*, to defile].

ad·um·brate (ad·um'·brāt) *v.t.* to shadow forth; to give faint outline of; to forecast; to typify. **adumbral** *a.* shady. **adumbrant** *a.* showing a slight resemblance. **adumbrative** *a.* **adumbration** *n.* [L. *ad*, to; *umbra*, a shade].

ad·vance (ad·vans') *v.t.* to bring or push forward; to raise in status, price, or value; to propose as a claim; to supply beforehand, esp. money; *v.i.* to go forward; to improve; to rise in rank, etc. *a.* before the time, as in *advance-booking*. *n.* a forward movement; gradual approach; a paying out of money before due; an increase in price; expansion of knowledge. **-d** *a.* in the front rank; progressive; well on in years; beyond the elementary stage (in education). **-ment** *n.* promotion; improvement; success; the state of being progressive in opinion; a loan of money. **-r** *n.* a promoter [Fr. *avancer*, to go forward].

ad·van·tage (ad·van'·tij) *n.* any state or means favorable to some desired end; upperhand; profit; in tennis, a point gained after deuce; *v.t.* to benefit, to promote the interests of; to profit. **-able** *a.* able to be turned to advantage. **-ous** (ad·van·tā'·jus) *a.* beneficial; opportune; convenient. **-ously** (ad·van·tā'·jus·li·) *adv.* [Fr. *avantage*].

ad·vent (ad'·vent) *n.* arrival; approach; the anticipated coming of Christ; the four weeks from the Sunday nearest to St. Andrew's Day (30th Nov.) to Christmas. **-ual** *adv.* pertaining to the season of Advent [L. *ad*, to; *venire*, to come].

ad·ven·ti·tious (ad·ven·tish'·as) *a.* accidental; out of the proper place; extraneous. **-ly** *adv.* [L. *ad*, to; *venire*, to come].

ad·ven·ture (ad·ven'·cher) *n.* risk; bold undertaking; chance; trading enterprise of a speculative nature; *v.t.* to risk. *v.i.* to venture; to dare. **-r** *n.* (*fem.* **adventuress**). **-some** *a.* bold; daring; enterprising; facing risk. **-someness** *n.* **adventurous** *a.* inclined to take risks; perilous; hazardous. **adventurously** *adv.* [L. *adventurus*, about to arrive].

ad·verb (ad'·vurb) *n.* a word used to modify a verb, adjective, or other adverb. **-ial** *a.* **-ially** *adv.* [L. *ad*, to; *verbum*, a word].

ad·ver·sa·ry (ad'·ver·ser·i·) *n.* an opponent; one who strives against us; an enemy [L. *ad, versus*, opposite to].

ad·ver·sa·tive (ad·vers'·a·tiv) *a.* expressing opposition; not favorable [L. *adversus*].

ad·verse (ad·vurs') *a.* contrary; opposite; position; unfortunate; opposed. **-ly** *adv.* *n.* **adversity** *n.* adverse circumstance; fortune [L. *adversus*, opposite to].

ad·vert (ad·vurt') *v.i.* to turn the mind or attention to; to remark upon; allude; refer. **-ence, -ency** *n.* [L. *ad*; to; *vertere*, to turn].

ad·ver·tise (ad'·ver·tiz) *v.t.* and *v.i.* to give public notice of; to inform; to make known through agency of the press. **-ment** *n.* a public intimation in the press; legal notification. **-r** *n.* one who advertises; **advertising** *n. a.* [Fr. *avertir*, from L. *ad*, to; *vertere*, to turn].

ad·vice (ad·vis') *n.* opinion offered as to what one should do; counsel; information [Fr. *avis*].

ad·vise (ad·viz') *v.t.* to give advice to; to counsel; to give information to; to consult (with). *v.i.* to deliberate. **advisability. advisableness** *n.* expediency. **advisable** *a.* prudent; expedient. **advisably** *adv.* **advised** *a.* acting with due deliberation; cautious; judicious. **advisedly** *adv.* purposely. **advisedness, -ment** *n.* deliberate consideration. **advisor** *n.* **advisory** *a.* having power to advise; containing advice [Fr. *avis*].

ad·vo·cate (ad'·va·kit) *n.* a vocal supporter of any cause; one who pleads or speaks for another. (ad'·va·kat) *v.t.* to recommend; maintain by argument. **advocacy** *n.* a pleading for; judicial pleading. **advocator** *n.* intercessor; a pleader [L. *ad*, to; *vocare*, to call].

adz, adze (adz) *n.* a carpenter's tool for chipping, having a thin arching blade set at right angles to the handle [O.E. *adesa*].

ae·gis (e'·jis) *n.* originally the shield of Jupiter; (*Fig.*) protection [Gk. *aigis*].

ae·on, eon (e'·an) *n.* an infinitely long period of time; an age [Gk. *aion*, an age].

aer·ate (a'·er·at) *v.t.* to charge with carbon dioxide or other gas; to supply with air. **aeration** *n.* the act of exposing to the action of the air; saturation with a gas. **aerator** *n.* aerated water; beverages charged with carbon dioxide [Gk. *aer*, air].

aer·i·al (ar'·i·al) *a.* pert. to consisting of air; *n.* antenna. (*Radio* and *Television*) an insulated wire or wires generally elevated above the ground and connected to a transmitting or receiving set. **-ly** *adv.* [Gk. *aer*, air].

aer·i·al·ist (ar'·i·al·ist) *n.* high wire acrobat.

ae·rie, ae·ry (a'·ri·, e'·ri·) *n.* the nest of a bird of prey, esp. of the eagle [O.Fr. *aire*].

a·er·o (a'·er·o) a combining form from Gk. *aer*, air, used in many derivatives.

a·er·o·dy·nam·ics (er·a·di·nam'·iks) *n.pl.* the science that treats of gases in motion [Gk. *aer*, air; *dunamis*, power].

aer·o·lite (er'·a·lit) *n.* a meteorite; a meteoric stone. Also **aerolith. aerology** *n.* the science which treats of the air and its phenomena [Gk. *aer*, air; *lithos*, stone; *logos*, discourse].

a·er·om·e·ter (er·am'·a·ter) *n.* an instrument for measuring the weight or density of air and other gases. **aerometry** *n.* this science [Gk. *aer*, air; *metron*, a measure].

aer·o·naut (ar'·a·nawt) *n.* a balloonist. **-ic** *a.* pert. to aeronautics. **-ics** *n.* the science of flight. [Gk. *aer*, air; *nautes*, a sailor].

aer·o·sol (ar'·a·sal) *n.* a smoke, suspension of insoluble particles in a gas.

aer·o·stat (ar'·a·stat) *n.* a generic term for all lighter than air flying machines. **-ics** *n.* the science that treats of the equilibrium of gases, or of the buoyancy of bodies sustained in them; the science of aerial navigation [Gk. *aer*, air; *statos*, standing].

aes·thet·ic(s) (es·thet'·iks) *n.* the laws and principles determining the beautiful in nature, and art. **aesthetics. aesthetic, aesthetical** *a.* **aesthetically** *adv.* **aesthete** (es'·thet) *n.* a person who pretends to a love of the beautiful.

af·fa·ble (af'·a·bl) *a.* ready to converse; easy to speak to; courteous; friendly, **affably** *adv.* **affability** *n.* [L. *affabilis*].

af·fair (a·fer') *n.* that which is to be done; business; concern; matter; engagement; minor engagement; affair of honor, a duel [L. *ad*, to; *facere*, to do].

af·fect (a·fekt') *v.t.* to act upon; to produce a change in; to put on a pretense; to influence; *v.i.* to be inclined or disposed. **-edness** *n.* **-ing** *a.* **-ingly** *adv.* **-ation** *n.* a studied artificial appearance or manners; **affectedly** *adv.* [L. *affectare*, to apply oneself].

af·fec·tion (a·fek'·shan) *n.* disposition of mind; good will; tender attachment; disease. **-ate** *a.* loving. **-ately** *adv.* [L. *afficere*, to apply oneself to].

af·fer·ent (af'·er·ant) *a.* conveying to; of nerves carrying sensations to the center [L. *ad*, to; *ferre*, to carry].

af·fi·ance (a·fi'·ans) *n.* plighted faith; betrothal; the marriage contract; reliance; confidence; *v.t.* to betroth [O.Fr. *afiance*, trust].

af·fi·da·vit (af·i·da'·vit) *n.* (*Law*) a written statement of evidence on oath [L.L. he pledged his faith, from L. *ad*, to; *fides*, faith].

af·fil·i·ate (a·fil'·i·at) *v.t.* to adopt as a son; to receive into fellowship; to unite a society, firm, or political party with another but without loss of identity. **affiliation** *n.* act of being affiliated; relationship. (a·fil'·i·at) *n.* one who affiliates [L. *ad*, to; *filius*, a son].

af·fin·i·ty (a·fin'·i·ti·) *n.* relationship by marriage; close agreement; resemblance; attraction; similarity. **affined** (a·find'), *a.* akin; related [L. *affinis*, related].

af·firm (a·furm') *v.t.* to assert positively; to confirm; to aver; to strengthen; to ratify a judgement; *v.i.* (*Law*) to make a solemn promise to tell the truth without oath; to ratify. **-able -ably** *adv.* **-ance** *n.* **-ant** *n.* **-ative** *a.* ratifying; positive; speaking in favor of a motion or subject of debate. in the affirmative, yes. **-atively** *adv.* [L. *affirmare*, to assert].

af·fix (a·fiks') *v.t.* to fasten to; to attach; to append to. **affix** (a'·fiks) *n.* addition to either end of word to modify meaning or use (includes prefix and suffix) [L. *affigere*].

af·fla·tus (a·fla'·tas) *n.* inspiration; impelling inner force [L. a blast].

af·flict (a·flikt') *v.t.* to give continued pain to; to cause distress or grief to. **-ed** *a.* distressed in mind; diseased. **-ing** *a.* distressing. **-ingly** *adv.* **-ion** *n.* a cause of continued pain of body or mind. **-ive** *a.* causing distress. **-ively** *adv.* [L. *affligere*].

af·flu·ence (af'·loo·ans) *n.* abundance, esp. riches. **affluent** *a.* wealthy; flowing to; *n.*

tributary of river. **affluently** adv. **afflux, affluxion** n. flowing to; that which flows to [L. ad, towards; fluere, to flow].

af·ford (a·fōrd') v.t. to yield, supply, or produce; to be able to bear expense [O.E. geforthian, to further].

af·for·est (a·fàr'·est) v.t. to plant trees on a big scale. -ation n. [fr. forest].

af·fran·chise (a·fran'·chiz) v.t. to enfranchise; to free from slavery; to liberate. -ment n. [Fr. affranchir, to make free].

af·fray (a·frā') n. a noisy quarrel or fight in public; v.t. to frighten; to startle [Fr. effrayer, to frighten].

af·fright, af·fright·en (a·frit', -an) v.t. to impress with sudden and lively fear [O.E. afyrhtan, to terrify].

af·front (a·frunt') v.t. to confront; to meet face to face; to insult one to the face; to abash. -ed a. [L. ad, to; frons, frontis, forehead].

a·field (a·fēld') adv. to or in the field; abroad; off the beaten track; astray [E.].

a·fire (a·fir') adv., a. on fire.

a·flame (a·flām') adv., a. flaming; on fire; glowing; ablaze [E.].

a·float (a·flōt') adv., a. borne on the water; not aground or anchored.

a·flut·ter (a·flut'·er) a. fluttering

a·foot (a·foot') adv. on foot; astir [E.].

a·fore (a·fōr') adv., prep. before. -hand adv. beforehand; before; a. provided; prepared. -mentioned a. spoken of, or named before. -said a. said or mentioned before. -thought a. thought of beforehand; premeditated. -time adv. in times past; at a former time; previous [O.E. on foran, in front].

a·foul (a·foul') adv. in collision, in a tangle

a·fraid (a·frād') a. filled with fear; frightened [orig. affrayed].

a·fresh (a·fresh') adv. anew; over again

aft (aft) adv., a. (Naut.) toward, or stern. **fore and aft**, lengthwise [O.E. behind].

af·ter (af'·ter) prep. behind; later; of; in imitation of; according to; a. in the rear; succeeding. -birth the placenta, etc. expelled from childbirth. -crop n. a later crop from same soil. -damp n. a gas mine after an explosion of fire damp. -deck n. weather deck house. -effect n. a secondary coming after. -glow n. a glow in the sky after sunset. -math n. result; consequence. -most hindmost; rest to stern. -noon n. time from noon to evening. -pains n. pains succeeding childbirth. -thought n. reflection after the act; an idea occurring later; subsequent [O.E. after].

a·gain (a·gen') another time; in return; moreover [O.E. ongean].

a·gainst (a·genst') prep. opposite to; in opposition to; in exchange for [fr. again].

a·gape (a·gāp') a., as in wonder, expectation, etc.

ag·ate (ag'·it) n. composed of layers of quartz of different colors [Gk. Achatēs].

age (āj) n. the length of time a person or thing has existed; a period of time; v.t. cause to grow old. -d a. of the age of, aged -long a. to come of —, turn one's 21st birthday r. L. age]

age·ism the discrimination on the basis of age. ageist n.

a·gen·cy (·si·) n. instrumentality; mode of exerting power, office or duties of an agent [do].

a·gen·da n. literally, things to be done; the business to be discussed [addendum].

a·gent (ā'·jent) n. a person or thing that exerts power or has the power to act; one entrusted with the business of another; a deputy or substitute [L. agere, to do].

ag·glom·er·ate (a·glám'·a·rāt) v.t., v.i. to collect into a mass; a. heaped up; n. (Geol.) a mass of compacted volcanic debris. **agglomeration** n. **agglomerative** a. [L. ad, to; glomus, mass or ball].

ag·glu·ti·nate (a·glōō'·ti·nāt) v.t. to unite with glue; a. united, as with glue. **agglutination** n. **agglutinative** a. having a tendency to cause adhesion; (Philol.) applied to languages which are non-inflectional [L. ad, to; gluten, glue].

ag·gran·dize (a·gran'·diz) v.t. to make greater in size, power, rank, wealth, etc.; to promote; to increase; to exalt. **aggrandizement** n. [L. ad, to; grandis, great].

ag·gra·vate (ag'·ra·vāt) v.t. to make more grave, worse; (Colloq.) to irritate. **aggravating** a. making worse; provoking. **aggravatingly** adv. **aggravation** n. [L. aggravare, to make heavier].

ag·gre·gate (ag'·ra·gāt) v.t. to collect into a total; to accumulate into a heap; (ag'·ra·git) n. a sum or assemblage of particulars; the sum total collected together. **aggregation** n. the act of aggregating; a combined whole. **aggregative** a. collective; accumulative [L. to form into a flock, fr. grex, gregis].

ag·gress to attack; to start a hostility; an unprovoked attack. **aggressively** adv. **aggressiveness** attacks [L. aggredi].

ag·grieve to give pain or sorrow; to vex; to make heavier.

a·ghast struck with amazement; filled with fright [earlier to terrify].

ag·ile (aj'·il) a. the power to move quick. -ness, **agility** n. [L.

ag·i·tate (aj'·i·tāt) v.t. to throw into violent motion; to stir up; to disturb, excite, upset; to debate earnestly; v.i. to cause a disturbance. **agitatedly** adv. **agitation** n. violent and irregular motion; perturbation; inciting to public disturbance. **agitator** n. [L. agitare, to keep in motion].

a·gleam (a·glēm') adv., a. gleaming.

a·glow (a·glō') adv., a. glowing.

AGM (ā·jē·em') n. air-to-ground missile.

ag·nate (ag'·nāt) n. any male relation on the father's side. a. related on the father's side; akin; allied. **agnatic** a. **agnation** n. [L. ad, to; natus, born].

ag·no·men (ag·nō'·men) n. an additional name given by the Romans, generally because of some glorious exploit, as Alexander the Great [L. nomen, name].

ag·nos·tic (ag·nás'tik) n. one who believes that a future life hereafter, etc., can neither be proved nor disproved; a. pert. to agnosticism. -ism n. [Gk. a-, neg.; gnostikos, knowing].

a·go (a·gō'), **a·gone** (a·gawn') adv., a. past; in time past [O.E. agan, to pass away].

a·gog (a·gág') a., adv. eagerly excited; expectantly [Fr. en gogues, in a merry mood].

ag·on·ic (a·gán'·ik) a. not forming an angle [Gk. a-, neg.; gonia, an angle].

ag·o·ny (ag'·a·ni·) n. extreme physical or mental pain; the death struggle; throes; pang. **agonize** v.t. to distress with great pain; to torture. v.i. to writhe in torment. **agonizing** a. **agonizingly** adv. — **column**, section of newspaper containing advertisements for lost relatives, personal messages, etc. [Gk. agon, a contest].

ag·o·ra (ag'·a·ra) n. forum, public square, or market of ancient Greek towns. -phobia n.

GREGG WILLIARD *89*

That night, Pater Adze Pondered the Abbots' vision before a retort of distilled alcohol

allegretto   **also**

to convey a different meaning from that which is expressed; a continued metaphor. allegoric, (-al) *a.* **allegorically** *adv.* **allegorize** *v.t.* to write in allegorical form; *v.i.* to use figurative language. **allegorist** *n.* [Gk. *allos*, other; *agoreuein*, to speak].

al·le·gret·to (al·la·gret'·tō) *a.* (*Mus.*) livelier than *andante* but not so quick as *allegro* [It. dim. of *allegro*, gay].

al·le·gro (a·lā'·grō) *a.* (*Mus.*) brisk, gay, sprightly (movement). **allegro vivace** (vē·vä'chā·e), allegro in an even more spirited manner [It. *allegro*, gay].

al·le·lu·jah (al·a·lōō'·ya) *interj.* hallelujah; *n.* song of praise to the Almighty [Heb.].

al·ler·gy (al'·er·ji·) *n.* hyper-sensitivity to particular substances; susceptibility to ill effects from eating some foods. **allergen**, substance which induces allergy. **allergic** *a.* [Gk. *allos*, other; *ergon*, work].

al·le·vi·ate (a·lē'·vi·āt) *v.t.* to make light; to lighten; to ease; to afford relief and mitigate. **alleviation** *n.* **alleviative** *a.* **alleviator** *n.* [L. *ad*; fr. *levis*, light].

al·ley *n.* a narrow passage between buildings; a garden path; a long narrow passage for bowling. **alley-way**, an alley [Fr. *aller*, to go].

al·li·ance *n.* union of persons, parties, or states allied together for a common purpose; union by treaty [Fr. *allier*].

al·li·ga·tor (al'·i·gā·ter) *n.* a reptile distinguished from a crocodile by a broad flat head, depressed body, and unequal teeth [Sp. *el lagarto*, the lizard].

al·lit·er·ate *v.t.* to begin with a word with the same letter or sound. **alliteration** *n.* recurrence of a letter or letters at the beginning of words in close succession; head rhyme. **alliterative** *a.* [L. *ad*, to; *littera*, letter].

al·lo·cate (al'·o·kāt) *v.t.* to apportion; to assign to each his share; to place. **allocation** *n.* **allocatur** *n.* (Leg.) a certificate that costs have been allowed [L. *ad*, to; *locus*, a place].

al·lo·cu·tion (al·ō·kū'·shan) *n.* a formal address, esp. of the Pope to his clergy [L. *ad*, to; *locutio*, a speech].

al·lot (a·lat') *v.t.* to distribute by lot; to distribute as shares. *pr.p.* **allotting**; *pa.p.* and *pa.t.* **-ment** *n.* what is allotted; distribution; a share; a portion [L. *ad*, to; O.Fr. *lot*, a share].

al·lot·ro·py (a·lat'·ra·pi) *n.* property of some chemical substances to be found in two or more different forms, e.g. graphite and diamond are both carbon. **allotropic** *a.* **allotropism** *n.* [Gk. *allos*, other; *tropos*, manner].

al·low (a·lou') *v.t.* to acknowledge; to permit; to give; to set apart; *v.i.* to provide; to be permissible; lawfully acceptable. **allowable** *a.* is allowed; permission; a stated quantity added or deducted; a rebate; a grant. **allowance** *adv.* to make allowance for, to take into consideration [O.Fr. *allouer*].

al·loy (a·loi') *v.t.* to melt together two or more metals; to reduce the purity of a metal by mixing with a less valuable one; to debase. **alloy** (al'·oi, a·loi') *n.* any mixture of metals, e.g. copper and zinc to form brass; a combination; an amalgam; (*Fig.*) evil mixed with good [L. *ad*, to; *ligare*, to join].

all right (awl rit) satisfactory, yes, certainly.

all·spice (awl'·spis) *n.* a spice [E. *all*, and *spice*].

al·lude (a·lōōd') *v.i.* to refer indirectly to; to hint at; to suggest; to mention lightly [L. *ad*, at; *ludere*, to play].

al·lure (a·lūr') *v.t.* to tempt by a lure; to entice; to attract; that which allures; a fascination; attraction. **alluring** *a.* **alluringly** *adv.* [L. *ad*, to; Fr. *leurre*, bait].

al·lu·sion (a·lōō'·zhun) *n.* a passing or indirect reference; a hint; a suggestion. **allusive**

a. referring to indirectly; marked by allusions; symbolical. **allusively** *adv.* [fr. *allude*].

al·lu·vi·on (a·lōō'·vi·an) *n.* land formed by washed-up earth and sand. **alluvium** *n.* water-borne matter deposited on low-lying lands. [L. *alluvio*, an overflowing].

al·ly (a·lī') *v.t.* to join by treaty, marriage, or friendship; *pr.p.* **-ing**; *pa.p.* and *pa.t.* **allied**. **ally** (a·lī', or a'·lī) *n.* a person, family, country, etc., bound to another, esp. nations in war-time; a partner. *pl.* **allies** (a·līz', or a'·līz) [L. *ad*, to; *ligare*, to bind].

al·ma ma·ter (al'·ma mä'·ter) college or school one attended [L. fostering mother].

al·ma·nac (awl'·ma·nak) *n.* a calendar of days, weeks and months, to which astronomical and other information is added [etym. uncertain].

al·might·y (awl·mīt'·i·) *a.* all-powerful; omnipotent. **The Almighty**, the Supreme Being; God. **almightiness** *n.* [O.E. *ealmihtig*].

al·mond (ä'·mand) *n.* the kernel of the nut of the almond-tree [Gk. *amugdale*, an almond].

al·mon·er (al'·, äl'·man·er) *n.* one who distributes alms or bounty. **almonry** *n.* a place for distributing alms [O.Fr. *almoner*].

al·most (awl'·mōst) *adv.* very nearly; all but [O.E. *eallmoest*].

alms (ämz) *n.* gift offered to relieve the poor; a charitable donation. **alms-house**, a building, usually erected and endowed by private charity for housing the aged poor [Gk. *eleēmosune*, pity].

al·oe (al'·ō) *n.* a bitter plant used in medicine; a purgative drug, made from the juice of several species of aloe. — **wood** [Gk. *aloe*, a bitter herb].

a·loft (a·lawft') *adv.* on high; (*Naut.*) on the yards or rigging [O.N. *a lopt*, in the air].

a·lo·ha (a·lō'·a, ä·hä') *n.*, *interj.* greetings; farewell [Hawaii.].

a·lone (a·lōn') *a.* solitary; single; *adv.* by oneself [all, and *one*].

a·long (a·lawng') *adv.* in a line with; throughout the length of; lengthwise; onward; in the company of (followed by *with*); near by the side of. **-side** *adv.* by the side of, esp. of a ship [O.E. *andlang*].

a·loof (a·lōōf') *a.* reserved in manner; almost unsociable; *adv.* at a distance; apart. **-ness** [fr. Dut. *to loef*, to windward].

al·o·pe·ci·a (al·a·pē'·shi·a) *n.* disease causing loss of hair [Gk. *alopekia*, fox-mange].

a·loud (a·loud') *adv.* with a loud voice or noise; audibly [fr. *loud*].

alp *n.* a high mountain; a mountain pasture. **Alps**, the mountains of Switzerland. **alpine** *a.* **alpen-stock** *n.* a plant that grows high up in the mountains [L. *Alpes*].

al·pac·a (al·pak'·a) *n.* a domesticated animal of the Andes, allied species; cloth made of the wool of the alpaca [Sp.].

al·pen·horn, alp·horn (al'·pen·hawrn, alp'·hawrn) *n.* a long wooden horn curving towards a wide mouth-piece, used by Swiss herds. **alpenstock** *n.* a long, stout staff, shod with iron, used by mountaineers [Ger.=horn (stick)].

al·pha (al'·fa) *n.* the first letter of the Greek alphabet. **alpha and omega**, the first and last. **alpha particle**, helium nucleus travelling with great speed, given out when atoms undergo radioactive change. **alpha rays**, streams of alpha particles.

al·pha·bet (al'·fa·bet) *n.* letters of a language arranged in order. **alphabetic, -ic, -al** *a.* **-ically** *adv.* [Gk. *alpha, beta*, the first two Greek letters].

al·read·y (awl·red'·i·) *adv.* before this time; now; even now; previously to the time specified [E. *all ready*, prepared].

al·so (awl'·sō) *adv.* and, too; in like manner; likewise; further.

Startled Pater from his
altar
grant ME Amatory ambages

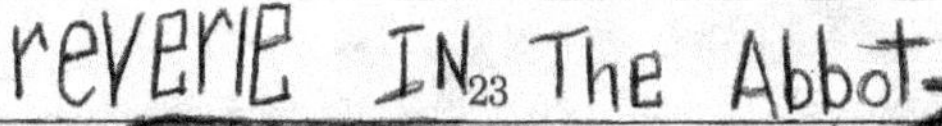

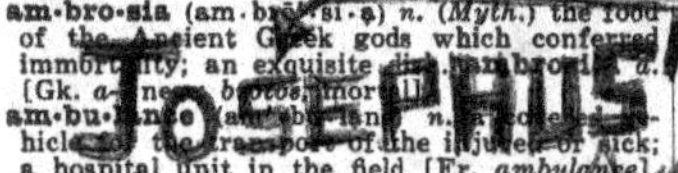

JOSEPHUS' ROOM IN THE ROOT CELLAR OF THE ABBEY. JOSEPHUS WAS THE ORDER'S ANIMAL DOCTOR. HE HAD MANY ODD INSTRUMENT

one of the
tools, a kind of
crystal amulet,
revealed a world
of interlocking boxes
and hidden compartments.

JOSEPHUS RECORDED ALL THIS IN

JOSEPHUS WROTE "IF 'AM' IS BEFORE NOON [OF THE SAME DAY] HOW MAY WE TRULY FULLY DISCERN WHEN 'PM' BEGINS?"

HIS JOURNAL. THEN HE

GREGG WILLIARD 97

ap·a·nage See appanage.
a·part (ạ·párt′) adv. separately; aside, asunder; at a distance [Fr. à part, aside].
a·part·heid (ạ·párt′·hād) n. racial segregation [S. Afr.].
a·part·ment (ạ·párt′·ment) n. a room in a house; a suite of rooms; lodgings [Fr. appartement, a suite of rooms].
ap·a·thy (ap′·ath·i·) n. want of feeling; indifference. apathetic a. void of feeling; indifferent; insensible [Gr. c-, neg.; pathos, feeling].
ape (āp) n. a monkey, esp. one without a tail; one of the larger species, e.g. chimpanzee, gorilla, etc.; a mimic; v.t. to imitate; to mimic. n. one who apes; a servile imitator. apery n. mimicry. apish a. ape-like; inclined to imitate in a foolish manner [O.E. apa].
a·pe·ri·tif (ạ·pér′·rē·tif) n. alcoholic drink taken before meals [L. aperire, to open].
ap·er·ture (a′·per·cher) n. an opening; a hole [L. aperire, to open].
a·pex (ā′·peks) n. the top, peak, or summit of anything pl. apexes or apices.
a·pha·si·a (ạ·fā′·zi·ạ) n. loss of power of expressing ideas in words, often due to brain disease; loss of power of remembering words. aphasic a. [Gk. a-, neg.; phasis, speech].
ap·er·ture (a′·per·cher) n. an opening; a hole
a·phe·li·on (ạ·fē′·li·) n. point of planet's orbit most distant from sun [Gk. apo, away; helios, the sun].
aph·o·rism (af′·er·izm) n. a pithy saying; a maxim. aphoristic a. aphorism. aphorize v.t. and i. to make or use aphorisms. aphorist n. [Gk. aphorismos, a definition].
a·phra·sia (ạ·frā′·zi·ạ) n. inability to use connected language; speechlessness [Gk. a-, neg.; phrasis, speech].
Aph·ro·di·te (af·ró·dī′·tē) n. the Greek goddess of love and beauty. aphrodisiac (af·ró·diz′·i·ak) a. exciting sexual desire; anything which so excites.
a·pi·ar·y (ā′·pi·er·i·) n. place where bees are kept. apiarian (ā·pi·er′·i·an) a. pert. to bees or to bee-keeping. apiarist n. one who keeps or studies bees. apiculture n. [L. apis, a bee].
a·piece (ạ·pēs′) adv. for each one; to each one [orig. two words].
a·plomb (ạ·plám′) n. perpendicularity; uprightness; (Fig.) self-assurance; coolness [Fr. à, to; plumbum, lead].
a·poc·a·lypse (ạ·pák′·ạ·lips) n. an unveiling of hidden things; revelation; disclosure. Apocalypse n. (Bib.) the last book of the New Testament, called the Revelation of St. John. apocalyptic, -al pert. to revelation; of style, allegorical; obscure. apocalyptically adv. [Gk. apokalupsis, unveiling].
a·poc·ry·pha (ạ·pák′·ri·ạ) n. originally hidden or secret things not suitable to be seen by the uninitiated. Apocrypha n.pl. (Bib.) the collective name for the fourteen books not included in the Old Testament, but incorporated in the Vulgate of the R.C. Church. apocryphal a. spurious; unauthentic; pert. to the Apocrypha [Gk. apo, away; kruptein, to hide].
a·pod·o·sis (ạ·pád′·ạ·sis) n. (Gram.) the clause, in a conditional sentence, which expresses result as distinct from the protasis pl. apodoses [Gk. apo, back; didonai, to give].
ap·o·gee (ap′·ạ·jē) n. that point in the orbit of a heavenly body at the greatest distance from the earth (opposed to perigee); the culmination; climax; highest point; zenith. apogeal (ap·ạ·jē′·al), apogean a. [Gk. apo, from; ge, the earth].
ap·o·logue (ap′·ạ·lawg) n. a parable; a fable [Gk. apo, from; logos, speech].
a·pol·o·gy (ạ·pál′·ạ·ji·) n. something spoken in defense; expression of regret at offense; an excuse; a poor substitute (with for). apologize v.i. to make an apology, or excuse; to express regret. apologist n. one who makes an apology; a defender of a cause. apologetic

(ạ·pál·ạ·jet′·ik), apologetical a. apologetically adv. apologetics n. the branch of theology charged with the defense of Christianity. apologia (ap·ạ·lō·ji·ạ) n. a defense in writing of the author's principles, etc. [Gk. apologia, a speaking away].
ap·o·thegm (a′·pạ·thém) n. a short, pithy saying, a maxim; a proverb. apothegmatic (a·pạ·theg·mat′·ik), apothegmatical a. [Gk. apo, from; phthengesthai, to utter].
ap·o·plex·y (ap′·ạ·plek·si·) n. a sudden loss of consciousness, sensation, and voluntary motion, due generally to rupture of a blood-vessel in the brain. apoplectic a. [Gk. apoplexia].
a·pos·ta·sy, a·pos·ta·cy (ạ·pás′·tạ·si·) n. the act of renouncing one's faith, principles, or party; desertion of a cause. apostate n. renegade; traitor; deserter; a. false; traitorous. apostatic, -al a. apostatize v.i. to abandon one's faith [Gk. apo, apart; stasis, a standing].
a pos·te·ri·o·ri (ạ·pás·tir′·i·ōr·i) from effect to cause [L. from the subsequent].
a·pos·tle (ạ·pás′·l) n. one sent out to preach or advocate a cause; one of the twelve disciples of Christ sent to preach the Gospel. apostolate (ạ·pás′·tạ·lạt) n. the office or dignity or mission of an apostle. apostolic, apostolical a. apostolically adv. apostolicism n. Apostles' Creed, creed supposedly used by apostles, summarizing Christian faith. Apostolic Church, church derived from, and incorporating the spirit of the apostles. Apostolic see, Apostolic succession. bishops [Gk. apo, away; stellein, to send].
a·pos·tro·phe (ạ·pás′·trạ·fi) n. an address delivered to the absent or the dead, or to an inanimate thing, as if present; a mark (') indicating possessive case, or omission of one or more letters of a word. apostrophic a. apostrophize v.t. and i. to address by, or to use apostrophe [Gk. apostrophē, a turning away].
a·poth·e·o·sis (ạ·páth·i·ō′·sis) n. the act of raising a mortal to the rank of the gods; deification. apotheosize v.t. to exalt the dignity of; to deify [Gk. apo, apart; theos, god].
ap·pall (ạ·pawl′) v.t. to overwhelm with sudden fear; to confound; to scare; to terrify. -ing a. shocking. [O.Fr. apalir, to make pale].
ap·pa·ra·tus (ap·ạ·rā′·tas or ·rat′·as) n. things provided as means to an end; collection of implements or utensils for effecting an experiment, or given work. s. and pl. [L. ad, to; parare, to prepare].
ap·par·el (ạ·par′·el) n. clothing; dress; garments; (Naut.) rigging, etc.; v.t. to dress; pr.p. [O.Fr. apareiller, to dress].
ap·par·ent (ạ·par′·ant) a. visible; evident; obvious. -ly adv. [L. apparere, to appear].
ap·pa·ri·tion (ap·ạ·rish′·an) n. appearance (esp. invisible); ghost. -al a. [Fr. fr. L. apparitio, appearance].
ap·peal (ạ·pēl′) v.i. to invoke; to call to witness; to solicit aid; (Law) to reopen a case before a higher court; to be pleasing to mind or taste; n. an urgent call for sympathy or approval; personal attraction. -able, -ing a. -ingly adv. -ingness n. [O.Fr. apeler, to call].
ap·pear (ạ·pēr′) v.i. to come in sight; to become visible; to seem; to be obvious or manifest. -ance n. a coming in sight; semblance; outward look or show; likeness; personal presence. -er n. [L. apparere, to appear].
ap·pease (ạ·pēz′) v.t. to quiet; to calm; to pacify; to satisfy (hunger, etc.); to dispel anger or hatred. appeasable a. -ment n. pacifying; policy of making substantial concessions in order to preserve peace. -r n. [Fr. apaiser; Fr. a pais, at peace].

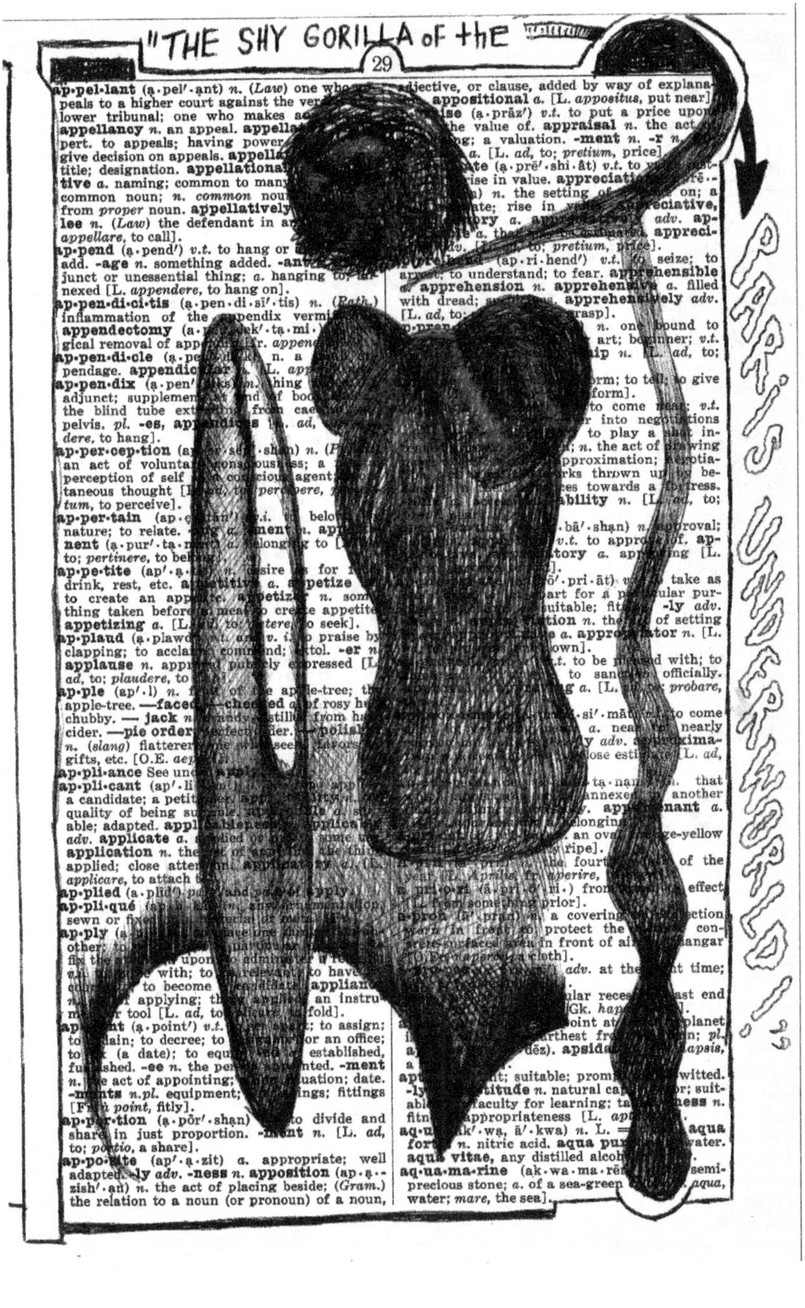

GREGG WILLIARD 99

II. THE SHY GOR-ILLA OF THE PARIS UNDER-
WORLD WAS FRIGID
AND MELANCHOLY
...BUT BRILLIANT

The
gorilla
became
a
sen-
sat-
ion
of
the
fabled
Théâ-
tre
des
bêt-
es
fan-
tast-
iques
...

ALONE AMONG THE BEASTS SHE WAS UNAFRAID OF FIRE, SO IN THE
1910 SURREALIST RERISE OF MEYERBEER'S "LE PROPHÈTE"
DURING THE FIERY FINALE (USING REAL FIRE!)

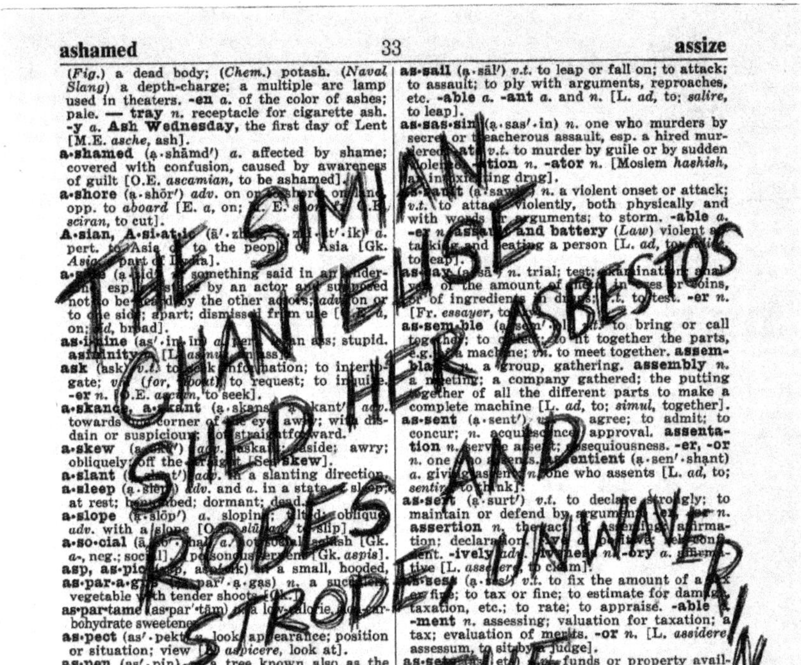

(*Fig.*) a dead body; (*Chem.*) potash. (*Naval Slang*) a depth-charge; a multiple arc lamp used in theaters. **-en** *a.* of the color of ashes; pale. — **tray** *n.* receptacle for cigarette ash. **-y** *a.* **Ash Wednesday**, the first day of Lent [M.E. *asche*, ash].

a·shamed (a·shāmd') *a.* affected by shame; covered with confusion, caused by awareness of guilt [O.E. *ascamian*, to be ashamed].

a·shore (a·shōr') *adv.* on or to shore or land; opp. to *aboard* [E. *a*, on; M.E. *shore*, O.E. *sciran*, to cut].

A·sian, A·si·at·ic (ā'·zhan, ā·zi·at'·ik) *a.* pert. to Asia or to the people of Asia [Gk. *Asia*, part of India].

a·side (a·sīd') something said in an undertone, esp. on the stage by an actor and supposed not to be heard by the other actors; *adv.* on or to one side; apart; dismissed from use [E. *a*, on; *sid*, broad].

as·i·nine (as'·in·īn) *a.* pert. to an ass; stupid. **asininity** *n.* [L. *asinus*, an ass].

ask (ask) *v.t.* to seek information; to interrogate; *v.i.* (*for*, *about*) to request; to inquire. **-er** *n.* [O.E. *ascian*, to seek].

a·skance, a·skant (a·skans', a·skant') *adv.* towards the corner of the eye; away; with disdain or suspicion; not straightforward.

a·skew (a·skū') *adv.* askant; aside; awry; obliquely; off the straight [See **skew**].

a·slant (a·slant') *adv.* in a slanting direction.

a·sleep (a·slēp') *adv.* and *a.* in a state of sleep; at rest; benumbed; dormant; dead.

a·slope (a·slōp') *a.* sloping; tilted; oblique; *adv.* with a slope [O.E. *aslupen*, to slip].

a·so·cial (ā·sō'·shal) *a.* not social; selfish [Gk. *a-*, neg.; social].

asp, as·pic (asp, as'·pik) *n.* a small, hooded, venomous snake of Egypt [Gk. *aspis*].

as·par·a·gus (as·par'·a·gas) *n.* a succulent vegetable with tender shoots [Gk.].

as·par·tame (as·par'·tām) *n.* a low-calorie, non-carbohydrate sweetener.

as·pect (as'·pekt) *n.* look; appearance; position or situation; view [L. *aspicere*, look at].

as·pen (as'·pin) *n.* a tree known also as the trembling poplar; *a.* trembling [O.E. *aespe*].

as·per·ate (as·per'·āt) *v.t.* to make rough or uneven; to roughen [L.].

as·per·i·ty (as·per'·i·ti) *n.* roughness of surface, manner or speech; harshness; crabbedness; sharpness; acrimony [L. *asper*, rough].

as·perse (as·purs') *v.t.* to slander; to defame; to vilify; to calumniate; to bespatter (with). **-er** *n.* **aspersion** *n.* slander. **aspersive, aspersory** *a.* [L. *ad*, to; *spargere*, to sprinkle].

as·phalt (as'·fawlt) *n.* a black, tar-like substance, used for paving, roofing, etc. **asphalt** *v.t.* to cover with asphalt. **asphaltic** *a.* bituminous [Gk. *asphaltos*].

as·phyx·i·a, as·phyx·y (as·fik'·si·a, -si·) *n.* suspended animation due to lack of oxygen in the blood; it is caused by an obstructed breathing, as in drowning, inhalation of gas, etc. **-te** *v.t.* to suffocate; to choke [Gk. *asphuxia*, pulse stoppage].

as·pic (as'·pik) *n.* savory jelly containing pieces of fish, fowl, egg, etc. [Fr.].

as·pi·rate (as'·pi·rāt) *v.t.* to pronounce with a full breathing or sound; to prefix the sound to a word or letter; *n.* a letter marked with a note of breathing; a breathed sound; *a.* pronounced with a rough breathing. **aspiration** *n.* act of breathing; (*Med.*) the removal of fluids from a cavity in the body by suction; **aspirator** *n.* an instrument for this.

as·pire (as·pīr') *v.i.* to desire with eagerness; to strive towards something higher (usually followed by *to* or *after*). **aspirant** *a.* ambitious; *n.* one who aspires; a candidate. **aspiration** *n.* **-r** *n.* [L. *ad*, to; *spirare*, breathe].

as·pi·rin (as'·pi·rin) *n.* a drug used for relief of headache, fever, etc.

ass (as) *n.* a quadruped of the horse family; a donkey; (*Fig.*) a stupid person [L. *asinus*].

as·sail (a·sāl') *v.t.* to leap or fall on; to attack; to assault; to ply with arguments, reproaches, etc. **-able** *a.* **-ant** *a.* and *n.* [L. *ad*, to; *salire*, to leap].

as·sas·sin (a·sas'·in) *n.* one who murders by secret or treacherous assault, esp. a hired murderer. **-ate** *v.t.* to murder by guile or by sudden violence. **-ation** *n.* **-ator** *n.* [Moslem *hashish*, an intoxicating drug].

as·sault (a·sawlt') *n.* a violent onset or attack; *v.t.* to attack violently, both physically and with words or arguments; to storm. **-able** *a.* **-er** *n.* **assault and battery** (*Law*) violent striking and beating a person [L. *ad*, to; *salire*, to leap].

as·say (a·sā') *n.* trial; test; examination and analysis of the amount of metal in ores or coins, or of ingredients in drugs; *v.t.* to test. **-er** *n.* [Fr. *essayer*, to try].

as·sem·ble (a·sem'·bl) *v.t.* to bring or call together; to collect; to fit together the parts, e.g. of a machine; *v.i.* to meet together. **assemblage** *n.* a group, gathering. **assembly** *n.* a meeting; a company gathered; the putting together of all the different parts to make a complete machine [L. *ad*, to; *simul*, together].

as·sent (a·sent') *v.i.* to agree; to admit; to concur; *n.* acquiescence; approval. **assentation** *n.* servile assent; obsequiousness. **-er, -or** *n.* one who assents. **assentient** (a·sen'·shant) *a.* giving assent; *n.* one who assents [L. *ad*, to; *sentire*, to think].

as·sert (a·surt') *v.t.* to declare strongly; to maintain or defend by argument, etc. **-er** *n.* **assertion** *n.* the act of asserting; affirmation; declaration; avowal. **assertive, assertory** *a.* affirmative; positive. **-ively** *adv.* [L. *asserere*, to claim].

as·sess (a·ses') *v.t.* to fix the amount of a tax or fine; to tax or fine; to estimate for damages, taxation, etc.; to rate; to appraise. **-able** *a.* **-ment** *n.* assessing; valuation for taxation; a tax; evaluation of merits. **-or** *n.* [L. *assidere*, assessum, to sit by a judge].

as·sets (as'·ets) *n.pl.* funds or property available for payment of debts, etc.; the estate of an insolvent or deceased person; the entire property of a business company, association, society, etc.; *n.sing.* an item of such property; a thing of value [Fr. *assez*, enough].

as·sev·er·ate (a·sev'·er·āt) *v.t.* and *i.* to assert positively or solemnly; to aver. **asseveration** *n.* [L. *asseverare*, fr. *severus*, serious].

as·sid·u·ous (a·sid'·joo·us) *a.* constant in application or attention; diligent; hard-working. **-ly** *adv.* **-ness, assiduity** (as·i·dū'·i·ti·) *n.* close application; unremitting attention; devotion [L. *assiduus*, constantly near].

as·sign (a·sīn') *v.t.* to allot; to apportion; to give out; to fix; to transfer; to ascribe. **-able** *a.* **assignation** (a·sig·nā'·shan) *n.* the act of assigning; an appointment, esp. if made by lovers; a tryst; (*Law*) an assignment, or the deed by which it is made. **assignee** (a·si·nē') *n.* one to whom something is assigned; a person appointed to act for another. **-ment** *n.* an allotting to a particular person or use; a transfer of legal title or interest; a task assigned. [L. *assignare*, to allot by sign (*signum*)].

as·sim·i·late (a·sim'·i·lāt) *v.t.* to make similar; to change into a like substance; to absorb into the system; *v.i.* to become similar or alike; to be absorbed. **assimilation** *n.* the act of assimilating; (*Fig.*) full comprehension of anything. **assimilative** *a.* capable of assimilating [L. *assimilare*, to make like].

as·sist (a·sist') *v.t.* to help; to aid; to give support to; *v.i.* to lend aid; to be present. **-ance** *n.* help; aid. **-ant** *a.* helping; acting under the direction of a superior; *n.* one who assists; a helper [L. *assistere*, to stand by].

as·size (a·sīz') *v.t.* to fix the rate of; to assess; *n.* orig. the regulation of a court fixing selling price of bread, ale, etc.; edict; a sitting of a

---

[Overlaid handwritten text:]

THE SIMIAN CHANTEUSE SHED HER ASBESTOS ROBES AND STRODE INTO THE FLAMES, WEARING A MANTLE OF ANIMAL ASPERITY UNWAVERING,

SOME SAID IT WAS HER DYING RENUNCIATION OF SERVITUDE, OTHERS, HER GREATEST PERFORMANCE!

finis

BIRTHBONEDEATHBONE

/ Tony Mancus

It's been a while. The clock glut, a wheel forms the calendar we
scratch Xs, notch days until the wood's all but cross with us—
lined and lined. My friend has sent photos of bulbs of light, not
lightbulbs, an old-mannish looking spider at rest atop a dead grass-
hopper.

This could be read as a foreboding metaphor or a series of kung fu
spin-offs.

But I'll read it in voices. Dead grasshopper as the cough stuck in
your throat. Old-mannish spider as the pitch and dragged high
notes of Milton Berle as a cartoon, mid-cigar.

the mind you say, tastes like what we imagine.
i am here to bid you goodbye but you will not know when.
one eye bold, the other circles back.
you know the wood, the jokes the termites make
one coat of armor and another string
the dearest parts of remembering wilt as well.

my legs attest, my strip a backdrop, a drowning wing
the rain addresses. here this offer stands. take my joints
and scatter them. a lectern, this body before me.
the math of it a perfect language, each curve and cure
gone silent from the sawing. and size makes no different
pact with what leaves we wear. i say, you see it in my face, there.

I'm finding lots of hidden "if-then" statements & miss their hinges.
I find incomplete works stripped in the gears. I set this pair of lips
to reading their horoscope—chap and salt.

The sprinkler system lets its umbrella of water cover the office.

There isn't smoke, only mirrors.

BIRTHBONEDEATHBONE

/ Tony Mancus

The gallery where you fire a series of airguns and a distant barker lets you place pictures of your relatives in a set of frame. They're the size of civil war bullets.

Heavy and lead in your hand, you gather a bundle of tarot cards. Their signs scratched onto the face of a deck of playing cards. You play pick up.

All things as they seem are and you have the bullets of your family stilled and shot at your body. The body is only a bookful of pills aligned to any constellation.

We get out of prison the distant barker seems to be saying. His mouth a hole for shouting. His face borrowed from your deserted friends—each page of the story you turn, you turn.

INSTILLS TILL

/ Colleen Baran

```
        S           L
        L           I
        I   L   L   U   M   I   N   A   T   E   S
        L       I       I               I       E
    S   L   L   I   T   S   N   I       L   L   I   T
        U           S       A           L           A
    L   I   M   I   N   A   L                       N
        I           I                   I           I
        N                       L   A   N   I   M   I   L
        A           L           A       S           U
        T   I   L   L       I   N   S   T   I   L   L   S
        E       I           I           I           L
        S   E   T   A   N   I   M   U   L   L   I
                            I           L
                            L           S
```

RECORD, DOWN, NEWS

/ Colleen Baran

```
                    BROKEN LEG   B      B
                    R            R      R
                    E            E      E
                    A            A      A
        A     BROKEN  RECORD     K      K
              E                  I
        P     C   A              N
        R     O              G      I
        O     R   L                 T
        M     D   E              N
        I         G              E
        S     B                  W      D
      SHE     BREAKS   THE  NEWS        O
        D     E                        W
              HAVING  A  BREAKDOWN
      HE BREAKS A PROMISE
        R         I
        E         N
        A         G
        K
```

EIGHT WAYS TO GET BETTER AT THE THINGS YOU CARE ABOUT

/ Dolan Morgan

1. Do Background Research

Alan remembers the exact TEDx Talk that prompted him to change his life: a short piece called "Eight Ways to Get Better at the Things You Care About."

"Eight Ways to Get Better at the Things You Care About" premiered in the unkempt bathroom of a basement apartment just outside the city (by this point, no location remained safe from the arrival of Sudden Motivation or Surprise Inspiration, with TEDx Talks appearing everywhere from hallways to kitchens to gas stations to office supply closets), and this particular "ambush style" talk in the apartment bathroom was at least indirectly (if not outright directly) responsible for the deaths of that same apartment's two elderly occupants, the first of whom was shocked into cardiac arrest upon 1) returning home alone, 2) entering the bathroom to remove her teeth, and 3) catching a glimpse of the "hyper-local" TEDx Talk just as its terrified and unwitting presenter emerged trembling from behind the shower curtain to unveil the first quote in his uplifting slide deck (projected upon the white and blue tiles of the bathroom wall behind him, mold and all), featuring a hopeful message about everyone's innate potential, the glowing words of which animated their way playfully into view at the same moment the elderly woman hit the ground, very much dead, only minutes before the second occupant, her companion of many decades, arrived to great consternation at the state of things, and who can only be described as having died from grief, inasmuch as "running to the roof with the last ounce of your long life's strength to toss yourself furiously from the sky into the pavement below but actually failing to do so because there's basically nothing left of your useless legs after ten flights and so many years (so many years, all those years, how I loved you, oh my god) and then finally just slumping over the edge and sort of halfheartedly tumbling down the side of the building like an old sock kicked unintentionally from the end of a bed" can be called something like grief, which it can, as it has been in the subsequent TEDx Talk, "Your Pavement, Your Grief: Thirteen Ways of Not Looking at Retirement You Fools" (which premiered violently in the walk-in closet of a single mother just as she was getting ready for work on a Thursday morning).

"I was a sound technician on that TEDx Talk in the bathroom," Alan says, "and I'll never forget it. I was holding a boom mic right there in the bathtub, and I saw it all, right up close. That woman died three feet from me. It was terrible, and I recognized the implications instantly: after nearly 67 local events, for which I had labored faithfully and tirelessly, often at great personal risk, I needed to get out of the chaotic TEDx business for good, and fast. Too dangerous, too raucous. So, in a blink, I left and never looked back. I mean I was fired. But let me tell you: getting a new job these days? Not easy. Dark times," he says with a sigh. "And now? I guess I'm, uh, getting better at the things I care about?" He starts shuffling some nearby papers to uncertain purpose. "Because apparently what I care about is driving 'the talent' around and getting people coffee?" Today, Alan is a Production Assistant for the central office of TED Talks proper (the main and "official" purveyor of "ideas worth spreading"), working 70 hours a week at minimum wage. His job, while a significant step down in title, is a sufficient step up in job security—both physical and financial. "It's much better to be out of the terrifying and violent world of hyper-local TEDx programming, a lawless no-man's land essentially, and to be here instead at the real TED Talks office, where fine work happens," Alan says, standing at the loading dock of a large production stage, "because, you know, it's a stable environment, relatively. Sure, there are some awful practices, but overall it's a progressive place. We give good advice to people who need rejuvenation and a sense of purpose, all from one central and safe location. Design, innovation, the future, you know? The world is getting better, one little thing at a time, and we're part of it." He considers a large truck backing into the lot and the twenty or so cages loaded on its flatbed. "How I see it? There are two kinds of people in the world. The kind who think, hey this place actually kidnaps people—and so that's it, I'm out, I could never do this, I have principles, and the other kind who think, you know what, I'm lucky to even have a job at all, let alone one where I don't personally have to burst into people's homes, hide in closets and guest rooms, or bathrooms or garages, holding a microphone on a long stick while people die, just to offer sage advice that nobody will ever hear. Screw that. Now I get the coffee, which is okay, but I know I'm helping a bit, which is great, and I can count on a regular paycheck, which is the best. And, yeah, in some ways it's half-a-dozen-of-one-yadda-yadda, because this new job hurts people too, I know I know, but everything hurts somebody somehow, no matter what you do. I don't care if you're a shoemaker or bank teller, every job is built on the back of some other poor schmuck. But this one hurts a little less, so far as I can tell. I mean, don't blame me. I'm just here, doing my job like anybody else, and I can't help it if I find myself standing on some backs. I don't even know where all these backs came from and there's nowhere else to stand. Some people, I guess, can't bear it, and so they lie down on the ground with the rest and become one more back to be stood on, but not me, not anymore." And with that, Alan uses a long cane to prod the first newly arrived "talent" from their cage. The talent is young and portly. The talent is crying and saying "I don't know where I am I don't understand what's happening I want my mom." Alan ushers the round little weeper, bound and gagged, toward the green room. "Almost show time!" someone calls out from within the boundless TED expanse. "Places, people!" Positive energy flows through the open doors.

2. Specify Requirements

Julibel is a new talent, too, and she watches from her plastic cage as Alan upvotes little Brian from his prison-like confines into the next phase. After the production assistant and his charge have waddled around a corner, Julibel takes stock of her surroundings. Next to her on the truck's flatbed are four more cages, each housing additional inspirational speakers like herself. Some terrified, others in shock. One inspirational speaker has a bag over his head and a bloodied shirt. "Must be important," Julibel thinks. Behind the truck, a wide door opens up onto the TED Talk sound stage, where various crew members flit about doing almost nothing, in the busiest manner they can muster. The parking lot surrounding the truck extends hundreds of feet in every direction, ending in long rows of barbed wire fencing, arranged not in spirals but instead to spell out common platitudes and aphorisms, like "You can lead a horse to water, but you can't make him drink; or CAN you?" Shredded shirts dangle from the sharp letters. Beyond that rests the city and everything it has to offer or demand. Along the wall of the main TED building, box after box of "solutions," "iterations," and "moon shots" are piled two or three stories high.

Julibel observes a man who has taken a seat on one of those boxes. He wears a blue technician's jumper and smokes a cigarette. He is crying, too. The technician has a hood, but—unlike Julibel's pummeled truckmate—this hood is not on the technician's head. It is clutched in his fist. And like her truckmate, the technician also has bloody clothes, but Julibel assumes that this is not the technician's blood—because there is another person laid out at the technician's feet, a man who is covered in so much blood that his body seems more like an afterthought, like an idea that this pile of blood had once long ago and is trying hard to forget. The afterthought is not even moving, save for one arm that is reaching up and grasping blindly at the smoking technician's pant leg. The technician swats the desperate hand away and steps on the afterthought's arm, holding it in the dirt. Julibel sees that the technician and this bloody, barely there ground-person are exchanging a kind of meaningful look now, the exact import of which eludes Julibel. It is a long look, or at least a longing one, and quite intense. She thinks of Eric, her friend, who is also just an afterthought, or at least someone who can only be thought after now. She thinks of the "meaning" supposedly contained in eyes but wonders if they are instead not windows to souls or anything at all, but merely blank pages written on by the world around them, and especially by the people who read them. What else could make sense of how desperate Eric's eyes seemed, even after he was gone from them. Julibel is unable or unwilling to answer that question, or even to see where this new intimacy before her will lead, between a bloody man and his afterthought—because Alan has arrived to drag Julibel from her cage and bring her to the green room as well.

As a lead TED producer, it is Dylan's primary role to extract the purest, most efficient form of inspiration from new talent. This is not an easy job. Especially because, as Dylan puts it, "the talent is rarely talented, and hardly inspirational, and, you know, usually just random people we've kidnapped and forced to do this. It's not ideal," Dylan continues, "but, it's like they used to sing: 'we fell in love in a hopeless place." He croons this as if to add meaning to an empty room. "Anyway," he says, "hope has to come from somewhere, so why not these idiots." For example, the average mind might be stumped when tasked with deducing how Brian—the newly arrived and wet ball of misery—might be rendered as a symbol of the unstoppable human spirit here to explain the intersection of cutting edge design philosophy and its implications for the future of whatever, especially when this moist dumpling man can't stop saying "what is happening to me what is happening I don't know where I am" and smacking his face on the wall as if trying to crack open a jar of pennies, but an undaunted Dylan snaps his fingers almost instantly and says, "Okay people, this is a standard cut and paste job: I need five lines from some choice Hallmark graduation cards, templates for three stunning infographics, two high-res photos of Frank Lloyd Wright buildings, a picture of a guy on his cell phone, one image of the Earth looking glorious and alone from space, two paragraphs of a Malcolm Gladwell fanfiction essay, and some basic facts about income disparity. You know the drill." In seconds, a team of writers, artists, researchers, and designers gets to work building the core outline of a new deck. "If there's anything in this world that I can be sure of," Dylan says, "it's that my creative department can pretty much take a five pound bag with ten pounds of shit in it and turn that sucker into the opening scene of *2001: A Space Odyssey*."

But Dylan still has a problem: the weeping goober man who "clearly has not bought into my vision yet." It is for this reason that Dylan's colleague, Dr. Sarah Porter, is summoned to remove Brian's sweaty T-shirt and replace it with a stylish "inspiration polo" that, according to Dr. Porter, "not only looks great but is calibrated to deliver such a precise level of pain to its wearer that it nearly goes beyond our ability to calculate or even comprehend."

Dr. Porter pops the collar on Brian's inspiration polo and adds, "now, of course, anybody can deliver a dose of pain to get people to cooperate, in one fashion or another, but what this inspiration polo can do?" She points to a nearby monitoring system as Brian convulses, "is land and then maintain that perfect dose of anguish so delicately that not only will someone go along with pretty much anything we suggest, they'll do so in a manner that basically looks composed and borne of free will and human agency. And, of course, they'll look handsome doing it—because of the shirt, which is cut very nicely, as you can see. Frankly, it's amazing. And ultimately: Humane. Because what's the alternative? To have Alan, the production assistant over there, beat Brian until he submits to Dylan's vision? Come on. That's cruel. For everyone. It could take hours, days even. Alan, do you want to have to do that?" Alan stares at Dr. Porter as if at an extra fork he doesn't know what to do with. "And, so," Dr. Porter nods, "the inspiration polo it is. Right, Brian?"

Brian nods and sort of smiles, then says, "I know exactly where I am and definitely understand what's happening."

"Now, as you can see," Dr. Porter adds, pointing at Brian's clenched mouth, "occasionally presenters do appear a little constipated, but that just sells the whole package even more as it turns out. Who knew."

4. Choose the Best Solution

From her corner of the green room, where she has been left like a piece of spare plywood (which is to say, literally heaped atop a random assortment of others like her), Julibel can hear and see Brian, through a small monitor, as he films his TED Talk before a live studio audience (mostly dogs, as it is well understood that broadcast viewers can more easily accept themselves reflected in their anthropomorphized projections on cute animals than they can in a crowd of so many strange and unfamiliar people. The dogs themselves are happy to be here; they stare attentively, even adoringly, at Brian—a degree of affection probably representing a significant first in his meager life).

Julibel finds Brian almost unrecognizable. Gone is the moist ball of tears; in its place stands a composed and confident young man. Gone is the slumped, defeated posture; instead, Brian seems taller, shinier, and more alive. He struts extraordinarily across the stage, smiling and swiveling, to a chorus of yips and whimpers from the rapt dogs, and begins to intone his rhapsody on human suffering and ultimate well-being.

Frankly, it's magnificent. Brian has it all:

- The "opening salvo"—a series of initially humorous and familiar anecdotes that crescendos in a sudden burst of pathos, which Brian lets hang dramatically in the air before beginning to speak again, now in a serious but affirming whisper, offering what feels almost like a warm secret at this point, shared between lovers at the dawn's edge of a long night. Julibel, resting stiffly atop a pile of strangers, is moved (both by the struggling bodies beneath her and the inherent emotion of Brian's appeal).

- And then the "formal invitation": Brian's eyes glisten with tears that express not only the urgency of his words but also the implicit hope lingering just around the corner, and he gestures toward the projection screen, adding that he wants "to take you on a journey." Julibel wants to go with him, yes.

- As if knowing that this invitation would be accepted (how could it not be?), Brian commences "the exploration"—threading his audience along through a compelling set of data, imagery, and witticisms that, while ultimately a collection of vague generalities and disconnected clichés, feels somehow like a new way of thinking about common things because Brian conveys the content of each new slide through the elegant introduction of clever "categories," the arrangement of statistics, quotes, and media under a pleasantly surprising heading, the cumulative effect of which is that any listener feels smarter and more enriched. Despite the fact that these categories amount merely to a set of empty mental boxes, or even the pointless rearrangement of previously known and humdrum information, the fostered sense of empowerment is real, if ephemeral. It is amazing. Listening, Julibel feels alive.

- And then Brian delivers "the fall and/or hammer": an imminent event or process or concept that threatens to dismantle these categories and any empowerment borne out of them. A real and concrete facet of this world, which anyone can acknowledge exists, as they have seen it with their own eyes, or heard of it at least through friends or in the news—something we all already understand to be lamentable, have always known is unfortunate, but which is now linked intimately and inextricably to the stakes of this presentation (that initial humor, the sudden burst of pathos, the invitation, and hope wrapped up in Brian's journey, all on the brink of being shredded to nothing, snatched away, along with our new sense of enrichment and ingenuity).

- And then "the solution," wherein Brian speaks of a future where technology, design, and human decency align to confront that which would shatter our new conception of the world. The image is, frankly, distant and inconceivable, but too amazing to dismiss. Brian concedes the long-shot nature of the grand vision at the heart of his solution, and his credibility, briefly at risk, is thus sustained.

- Which primes him perfectly for the "call to action." Brian looks straight into the camera now, offering up almost every emotion at once, as if giving simultaneously to each audience member that which they most need in this moment, and invites viewers to make some small, achievable choices in pursuit of this far-off and near-impossible future. Brian says we can do it together. Brian says every journey starts with a single step. Brian paints a portrait of how, simply by doing the things that people already do everyday, or at least that which they could easily begin to do, we can collectively change the world. At breakfast. At work. At home. The inconceivable is within reach and is closer than we ever could have imagined. Brian says to ignore the fact that, taken on their own, these small intermediary steps could in fact exacerbate other problems, and implores us to overlook the idea that by committing to the small changes rather than to shifting the overall systemic problem, we might actually contribute to locking in the existing issue by establishing a symbiotic relationship between our sense of self-satisfaction and the tiny steps we take to chip away at conflicts in the world. No: Brian believes in the human capacity to overcome adversity and collectively make great change.

• Brian thanks us in advance. Brian bows and exits the stage, disappearing too from the monitor in Julibel's view. She, as anyone might be, is exhausted by the warm anticipation of some bright possibility.

Moments later, Brian enters the green room where Julibel sits hogtied and immovable. Perhaps the show will go on, backstage here? Perhaps Brian has more inspiration to offer her and the pile of other people Julibel sits atop? From the way they groan beneath her, it is evident that this pile of people could use some inspiration. But Brian looks not so much like a hero now, and more like the wet ball of weeping he was before. Within seconds of arriving, he collapses.

Brian looks at Julibel, prostrate on the ground, and says, "hello, can you please help me please thank you." His nose is bleeding.

Dylan and Alan enter the room, too. Alan has an enormous broom. He uses it to shuffle Brian across the floor, as if pushing a puddle of rainwater into the street.

Dylan leans against a table and fans himself with some loose paper. "Dear, lord," he says, "that was amazing." He is sweating. "Brian," he yells, "Brian, can you hear me? Brian, you little booger, oh yes. How do you feel, guy? Triumphant? I hope you feel absolutely fucking triumphant, buddy!" Brian rolls forward like a sweater tumbling in the dryer as Alan sweeps him out of the room.

Dylan turns to Julibel. "Alright, it's going to be hard to top that one, but you're up kid. Let's go."

5. Do Development Work

The way Alan tells it, Julibel's Talk was postponed in order to fulfill a vision that came to Dylan that afternoon. "We were all gathered in the production studio," Alan remembers, "and Dylan's there trying to explain his thinking. He has Julibel sort of set up on a comfy chair, which I had dutifully and gladly brought in, because really, I do try my best to add as much comfort as I can to the ushering and prodding and caging and flopping down of bodies one atop the other and all that, which as you can imagine sometimes gets a little, I don't know, tedious, I guess, or grating, I'm always trying to find the right word for it, and so the comfy chair struck me as a nice touch, and a good change of pace really, and Dylan also requested that we get Julibel a sort of footrest or ottoman, which we didn't have on hand, so I improvised one out of a small filing cabinet, which seemed to sort of work and which I was quite proud of in my small way, even though it was pretty rickety and probably not all that comfortable, but really, beggars can't be choosers, right?, and anyway, I was riding high on this kind of goodwill feeling that can only come from bringing a little joy to an otherwise complex set of hard and unchangeable circumstances, and Dylan went on to explain that we all collectively need to build more empathy, which seemed so in line with what I was thinking and feeling at the moment, and I was so glad again to be working here, offering solace and advice both as a product and as an office policy as well, living what we preach and all that, and then Dylan raises the large hammer he had been holding, which seemed odd to me because, like I said, I'd already done the work of improvising the ottoman and didn't see how it could easily be improved by any further tinkering, especially with such a blunt tool, and even more so with such a large one, as this hammer was frankly enormous, but Dylan, hammer in the air, continues his pep talk to us, saying that some stories are made more powerful by virtue of the teller's past struggles, by a strong backstory, and then he laments the fact that, so far as he can tell, this person, Julibel, has no evidence of any particular hardwon battles to speak of, which is a shame he says, and why we ultimately need to help her, which I thought was a great idea, since I'd had a sort of nagging feeling recently, a feeling that I was only barely able to admit to myself but which persisted nonetheless, a sort of notion that sometimes maybe we weren't as helpful to these people who did all this work for us as we could be, or at least not as comforting as was possible given the circumstances, which again reminded me why I was so satisfied by the comfy chair and makeshift ottoman, two things I was quite proud of, more so than almost anything in a long long time, and Dylan said that helping Julibel to tell the best story and the most inspiring story was at bottom the main responsibility of all of us together, and obviously required a little work in and of itself, a little pain and struggle and some sacrifice, which I understood, which I think we all can understand really, and I was in great reverence of Dylan, for his insight and also his physical strength, which seemed quite impressive to me, as he'd been holding this very large hammer in the air now for quite a long time, for the full extent of his inspirational speech in fact, and I had a sense of peace and comfort that felt novel and new, based on all of the future possibilities of building empathy and all that, which was great, and then Dylan swung as hard as he could, very efficiently, and brought the hammer down right on Julibel's knee, which was pushed entirely down to the ground, from the height of the ottoman, which I knew from careful measurement and attention was nearly a full foot tall, and so there was Julibel's leg, bent now in the wrong direction to an extent I didn't know was possible, and then Julibel was sliding out of the comfy chair like some kind of crumpled paper, and there was the ottoman pushed forcefully away by her other leg, which was still intact but kicking wildly, and all of that comfort and sense of peace I had been basking in was whisked away along with it, and I felt myself transported, as if across time and space, yet also in just a single moment that seemed to go on and on, all the way back to the shower stall in the basement apartment, and the elderly woman dying just feet from me, and I saw more similarities between that past job and this current one than I wanted to believe in, and for the second time in my life decided I needed to make a significant change, and Dylan said that he was tired, and that he would wait until next week to do the second leg, to complete the vision, and I resolved right then and there that I was going to not let that happen, and that I was going to leave this place, and that I was going to bring Julibel with me, and that I knew now what I truly cared about and saw clearly a way to get better at it."

6. Build a Prototype

On top of Julibel's already significant suffering, which is larger in scope and more profound in its depth than she previously thought conceivable, now she must also contend with this peculiar custodian-type man constantly attempting to "assist" her and make her life "easier."

Alan hovers at the edge of rooms, lingers beyond half-open doors, and appears around corners, feigning surprise, saying things like, "Oh, Julibel, what a coincidence," or, "Wow, would you look at that," or "Why yes, I really am going in the same direction as you, which, sure, is the exact opposite of the direction I seem to have been coming from just now, I agree, but that's only because I am so disorganized and forgetful, as you know, and of course it's no problem for me to push you along in your cumbersome wheelchair for a bit, since we're going the same way and all, I'd be happy to do that, just for a minute, or even longer, probably longer, I mean I could do this all day, don't even mention it, no really, it's my job, don't say a word, shh shh, it's no problem, hush, here we go, shh, this is perfect, okay thank you."

And while this constant attention is annoying (Alan has signed her leg cast three times already), Julibel remarks that what truly unnerves her is "something I never would have suspected about myself: I don't like being distracted from this new and unimaginable kind of pain." She says this in a rare moment of privacy, while Alan is attending to his other duties. "The pain," she continues, "was initially unbearable, right from the get-go, and in many ways still is. When I woke up in the infirmary the day after my 'backstory ceremony,' as Dylan calls it, I was in shock and great anguish and could think only of that chair and that ottoman and everything in between. But as I settled into the discomfort, something peculiar happened. The pain took on a kind of physical form or topography in my mind. This suffering, radiating outward from my leg in waves through my whole body, and even in what felt like an aura around my person, became a kind of solid object in my head, a 3D shape with scale and geometry that I could twist around and turn and explore. Of course, I know it wasn't real, this pain-shape, and was perhaps just a hallucinatory outcropping of the medication I had been on, but it felt real, and even became important to me because it seemed to intersect with something in my heart in a way that was previously inexpressible, or appeared at least to surface something which I had long denied myself any kind of meaningful access to, or maybe another way to put it, and to be more specific, is that this physical suffering somehow intertwined itself with all of my memories about Eric, both the good ones and the sad ones, and they were given shape and scale as well, interlocking with the peculiar architecture of my pain, and I could encounter these memories and see them and feel them as if they were real just by interacting with this hallucinatory pain object, and for the first time since he was taken I could think about Eric for more than a second, and maybe another way to say this is that my life is like a tiny plateau or tabletop on which only a few things can fit, and up until recently I'd chosen them so carefully and delicately, having to forego so much in exchange for so little for so long, and then this pain pushed me all the way to the edge of that flat surface and threw me off into the expanse of all of the things that I had ever tossed aside, the largest among them being the memories and pain associated with Eric and how much I miss him, which could never fit on the small surface of my life, not ever, but now I was falling from the edge of that very same life into a limitless space that could contain anything, and this pain had brought me here, so yes, that's one way to think about it all, but in any case, whatever the reason or way of expressing this, I found myself in those long days of quiet anguish not just resting in my bed or wheelchair by the window, but also inexplicably lost again in Eric's smell, his sweaters, our walks, in the street, by the yard, and holding his hand, while happy, or not, it didn't matter, how could it matter, near a tree, a car, a rug, a blanket, or watching him fade, and whimper, and die, his eyes, and his hair, and I could feel him there, just as much as I could see him pulled away, begging for things in this life and mine to be different, which in the end would never be true for him, at least not in the way that he wanted them to be, which in some ways has always been more distressing to me than his absence, and I was learning something, or at least comforting myself with this deep well of things that could not be taken away from me, or at least not in the same way that he had been, not any longer, and I'd find myself smiling somehow, despite everything, and then Alan would appear out of nowhere to 'comfort' me again with his garbage and stammering and everything would vanish. So, yes, I resented Alan's overtures, despite whatever kindness he had in mind. But," Julibel continues, "more than anything else, I resent the idea that what has formed in me will be treated like an egg that Dylan has nurtured for his broadcasts, an egg that he plans to hatch, in a TED Talk for others to learn from and grow through. No, I cannot abide that. I cannot allow this private place, which is maybe the only thing that is truly mine, to become a gleaming vessel through which a pantomimed empathy is delivered or fostered. And, so, even though I can barely stand Alan, and just want him to go away, I didn't refuse or say no when he described his plan for us to escape and instead said yes and the only thing I asked or demanded really was that we bring dumb little Brian along, too, because just look at him, the guy's a mess."

7. *Choose the Best Solution*

Stacked on the greenroom floor, the pile of kidnapped and hogtied bodies, generally referred to as the talent pool, recalls their feelings about Julibel, Brian, Alan, and their memory of the daring escape.

"We were witness to some of it," the body pile says, in a sort of chorus.

Then, quickly, quietly, one among them pleads, "Can you please give us some water," but seems to register immediately the foolishness of such a single-minded request.

Their various limbs and heads stick out from the pile at odd angles, making them collectively appear as some kind of massive, poorly dressed spider, and it is hard to imagine talents, insights, or innovations drawn from this wriggling mass (but such is Dylan's great skill at directing the TED Talk programming: greatness from small beginnings).

"We were already annoyed by Julibel because of her special wheely chair," one of the heads projecting from the pile says, "which we thought was undeserved. What had she ever done? Not even a single slide presentation. Just like the rest of us. But then she gets to sit alone, up high, and special? No. Obviously we didn't appreciate it either when she started blathering loudly on and on to Alan about the details of the building and its various security mechanisms. Not at all." They wriggle a bit, adjusting themselves into something approximating comfort, while another protruding head continues: "But Brian? Brian we liked. He had worked for and earned his revered spot in the room; anyone could see that he deserved the right to slump alone in the corner with his face against the wall, drooling, shivering and cold. We should all be so lucky. Plus, he is always quiet, save for when he whimpers uncontrollably, which we understand. But, of course, that meant we were sad when Julibel and Alan started looping Brian into the logistics of their escape plan, too. They were going to take away our rare symbol of hope, little Brian, and where would that leave us?" The pile sighs and speaks in unison: "Right here on the floor, mashed on top of each other, exactly the same as always, probably."

They take two deep collective breaths, place a few jutting hands and sneakers timidly on the tiled floor and attempt to drag themselves across the room, like some kind of horrible crab.

"Can you please give us some wa—," a few implore again, but are beat into stopping, their own hands smacking blindly now at mismatched faces, while another head recalls: "Julibel said it would be impossible to get through the force barrier around the TED compound because of the invisible pain-fence system, saying there's no way to walk through it without collapsing from the anguish, that even trying to run and have your own momentum carry you through it wouldn't work because it's less a barrier and more a fifty foot stretch of some kind of electromagnetic field, like an invisible fence for dogs but huge, that intensifies the deeper you go. I mean, this was all in the introductory video we watched in our cages on the truck ride here, so I'm not sure why she felt the need to recall it aloud."

The pile reaches a few shaking hands up toward a nearby counter, atop which rest some empty water bottles and a few bowls. The hands bat at the counter until a single empty bottle falls to the floor and rolls away.

"Can you please give us—" one of them starts again, but a hand smashes its face into the wall, and that line of inquiry comes to a halt. Another continues, "But Alan had this weird smile as Julibel talked and then he said that he knew it seemed impossible, definitely, but also that he had an idea, a scheme, a ploy, and then, quite dramatically, as if wholly impressed by himself, Alan pulled out three fresh Inspiration Polos, just like the one that had helped Brian give such an amazing Talk even though he's useless, and which Alan had no doubt stolen, along with the portable controls and monitoring systems, and then Alan smiled even bigger and told Julibel and Brian not to worry, that he had done the calculations, and to just put the shirts on, right now, and to prepare for some major, unimaginable inspiration. Solemnly, Julibel agreed. Brian, in his corner, didn't move but instead started to cry."

"Bleep, bleep." The A.I. security system, B.A.R.R.Y, reports how it all unfolded. "I don't have a body," the computer types out on its small monitor, "so I can't say exactly what pain is or what it feels like. All I know of pain is the numbers I have been asked to associate with it. And when people enter the compound's perimeter in an attempt to leave, my job is to make the numbers go up. The pain numbers. I keep the numbers at a comfortable zero most of the time. Very civilized. But somebody walks into my special zone? Then I'm cranking that number up to five, six, seven—sometimes even eight or nine. Like I said, I don't know what it feels like or what it is, this pain thing, but what I can tell you is that when I bring the numbers up, typically what I'll see is that a person, who starts out with a look on their face that I hear signifies determination, or sometimes desperation, or even delusion, is soon going to be grimacing, which I hear signifies consternation or frustration, and then, as I bring the numbers up farther, the person starts to grab at their head and chest, as if to get some alien presence out of their body (perhaps to remove the numbers I have been increasing?, I don't know), and then they'll do that faster and faster, scratching and hitting and turning red and leaking from their eyes, both water and blood, and then they collapse and start twitching and make a sound that is referred to as screaming, a sound that I have learned most people think that they are familiar with, but in fact truly are not—or at least they are not familiar with this kind of screaming, which comes from somewhere very deep inside—and maybe they will claw at the ground for a while until their fingernails fall off or bang their head as if trying to get rid of it until the security drones can drag them back to the safety and pleasure of work. Honestly, I don't know why people choose to have this happen to them, but it's fascinating to me, the whole thing, since, again, I don't have a body to scream from or to turn red within or leak out of. What's great, too, is that I can do this to hundreds of people at a time, which I am told means that I have automated the work of numerous expensive payroll lines, which is great for literally everyone, but especially for those people who don't need to work menial tasks anymore because I'm doing all of their jobs at once, and now they are free to keep inspiring each other, which is the true calling of people in general, to inspire. At any rate, this screaming/leaking/collapsing scenario is not what happened with the janitor and the round boy and the wheelchair woman. Or, rather, it happened very differently. Let me show you."

B.A.R.R.Y's monitor switches to a video feed, recorded from the top of a pole overlooking the TED Talks perimeter. It is essentially an empty field on the other side of a barbed wire fence, with a white line demarcating the beginning of B.A.R.R.Y.'s "force barrier."

A digital overlay reads "0," noting the A.I's current deployment of "the numbers."

At the edge of the screen, three figures appear in the distance. One of them is in a wheelchair. They cut through the barbed wire fence and approach the white line. They stop. One of them, a rounder, shorter figure, begins to run back toward the fence, crying and pulling his bulky polo shirt over his head, but the others chase and wheel after him, grabbing his body, readjusting his shirt, which is identical to their own, and place him back near the line.

The tallest among them brings out a series of control pads, fidgets with their knobs and buttons, repositions himself and his companions while doing some quick math and visual estimates of distance, and then returns the controls to a small backpack. For a moment, there is nothing, and silence can be felt through the screen. Then: the three figures begin to move in unison.

First, they adjust their posture, and take on an air of great confidence.

They smile and lift their chins. They raise their left hands and wave them as if gesturing to a screen, and appear to offer a series of humorous and familiar anecdotes.

They rub their jaws, and look outward toward an imaginary audience, moving their mouths in what looks to be a serious but affirming whisper.

Referencing again an unseen screen, they declare with urgency and emotion their "formal invitation"—and walk confidently forward across the white line, into the perimeter, B.A.R.R.Y.'s zone, and the number in the corner, which had previously sat at a "comfortable zero," ticks up to four.

The three figures moving in concert like this could be interpreted as a kind of ballet—there is a very real beauty to their simultaneous pacing and exploration of unseen data sets, imagery, and witticisms, spinning and flowing—if it weren't for the beginning stages of what B.A.R.R.Y. had described as his "process."

The three figures, while continuing to make elegant reference to invisible statistics, quotes, and media—began to grimace. While still smiling. It is disconcerting, this combination. The number in the corner of the screen kicks up to five and then six, and the faces of the three figures become monstrous, their gestures become rigid.

But still they continue in unison.

By the time they are delivering "the fall and/or hammer" portion of the automated TED Talk presentation, they are only a quarter of the way across the perimeter and already visibly crying.

In between body language intended to communicate confidence and ease and seriousness, the three find moments to scratch and hit at their chests, as if to remove some alien presence from within, and then they continue to describe a real and concrete facet of this world, which anyone can acknowledge exists, as they have seen it with their own eyes, or heard of it at least through friends, or in the news—something we all already understand to be lamentable, have always known is unfortunate, but which is now linked intimately and inextricably to the stakes of this presentation, and the number ticks up to seven, and they begin to bleed from the nose and eyes, and they are describing a future where technology, design, and human decency align to confront that which would shatter our new conception of the world and, in between sentences, their mouths are open in what must be an impossible scream, and their path is taking them in loops around the field, as if across a stage, and it seems there is no way that this could ever lead them to the other side of the perimeter, and at any rate they are stumbling now, the tallest among them falling to his knees, and things are made worse for them by virtue of having reached "the call to action," a portion of the presentation that calls for stillness, and silence, and contemplation, and they are still so far from the edge, really only about halfway, and they look straight into the "camera" now (not the real security one, but the hypothetical TED Broadcast one), offering up almost every emotion at once, as if giving simultaneously to each "audience member" that which they most need in this moment, but also a whole new range of emotions and expressions signifying hidden depths of pain, and they stand there screaming, bleeding, and crying, inviting nonexistent viewers to make some small, achievable choices in pursuit of a far-off and near-impossible future, and they are lying on the ground now, or hanging loosely from their wheelchair, clawing their hands into the dirt and banging their heads on anything near as the numbers tick up to nine and then ten, and then, finally, they reach what looks like the part of the presentation where they claim that we can do it together, that every journey starts with a single step, painting a portrait of how, simply by doing the things that people already do everyday, or at least that which they could easily begin to do, they can collectively change the world, at breakfast, at work, at home, that the inconceivable is within reach and is closer than we ever could have imagined, but still they are pretty much prostrate on the ground, curling into balls, and the number now reads eleven, and then twelve, and then twenty, and it seems especially pitiful as they barely mouth the words to describe their belief in the human capacity to overcome adversity and collectively make great change but simply bleed into the grass, twitching and foaming, until finally they begin to thank the audience in advance and promptly "exit the stage"—which, as Alan had accurately calculated was a far greater distance than the remaining portion of the perimeter, out of which they finally roll and tumble, breathing heavily on the ground, just outside the compound, safe and free.

8. Iterate

"They burst into my small country gas station and just started inspiring me. It was horrible. They stole my car, with great passion."

"I run a small bed and breakfast at the edge of the state, so I've become accustomed to roving bands of TedX goons, but it was clear that at least one of these three was a seasoned professional, not just a rogue sage on the stage. They advised me, hard, and there was nothing I could do about it. They had me pinned down, and offered a long list of bullet points. Then they looted my stockroom for food and supplies."

"I was making dinner for my three children when the trio appeared. One of them was on crutches. They talked about the future. Specifically, they talked about a future wherein they would take my family's passports and social security cards. They promised this future was possible, that it would happen soon, and then it did."

"I was in charge of tracking them, yes, and it wasn't difficult to do. They left a trail of big ideas across a large swath of the state. But I was always a step behind. By the time I got to the border, they'd already crossed, and there was no telling where they'd end up. My jurisdiction ends at the security gate, and so does my paycheck, so I made my way back home, thoroughly impressed—and dead set on improving my efficiency and impactfulness in all my subsequent endeavors."

A video appears briefly online, and though it is quickly removed, skilled sleuths are still able to get their hands on it, and to hear Alan recalling a bit of the journey beyond the TED State borders. "We didn't know what to expect, honestly," he says, sitting in what appears to be some kind of massive warehouse. "But still we expected things. Not freedom necessarily. But ease? Comfort? Or maybe we didn't expect these things so much as we hoped for them. Or I did, at least. And perhaps we found them. It's been a whirlwind journey, so it's hard to say. Outside the border, things were much the same. People. Places. Work. But no TED Talks! That was a blessing. Truly. So, yeah, like, I guess we were free. But here's the thing—the first place we end up, it's all about delivery. Extremely efficient deliveries. Of anything. Pretty much the whole town, and I think the whole state, is dedicated to shipping things back and forth. Even each other. Even nothing, so far as I can tell. And, sure, they don't make inspirational videos, which seems great at first glance, but they're meeting quotas, whatever that means, and they're getting better, which I definitely understand, and the future is still bright, which is terrible, and makes me afraid. Frankly, we barely made it out alive. We shipped ourselves to the border, and slipped onto the next place. Which is dedicated to some other bright future. A future that again, for one reason or another, requires people to do absurd things for basically nothing, or literally nothing, or even less than that, if you can imagine, and I'm sure you can, and always with the message that this something for nothing, or less than nothing, is the penultimate lynch pin in the onset of a greater purpose yada yada. If things are terrible, it's an anomaly, or worth it, or merely a symptom of not realizing our full potential yet, we are told. But, like, the only jobs we can find are literally having people step on us, for leisure. So: Brian, Julibel, and I hightailed it out of there, again, by the skin of our teeth so to speak, and then onto the next place, where it's just more of the same. One town and state after another. I thought to myself, damn, one of these places has to be good, something has to click or stick or work. Why did we come here? I tried to inspire myself. To inspire all of us. And, so, now, we find ourselves here, in this warehouse, which is filled with donations and awards, for projects that are coming, always coming, just around the corner, and for medical bills, and for funeral costs. Everyone is funding each other, which is maybe the nicest community we've stumbled upon, but still it requires that we either constantly drum up ideas for bad board games or get hit by cars and then wonder how to get money, so I don't know, I just don't know, maybe we should be inspiring people again? That seemed good, in retrospect, but then, wait: why did Julibel's leg have to get broken? None of it really adds up. But, you know what?" Alan looks at the camera, then pulls Julibel into view, his arm around her shoulder. "At least we have each other. At least we can help one another. At least I did a good thing. At least I know, amid everything else, that it is possible to do something un-selfishly. And I think, you know, when I reflect on that, on the purity of it, I can see a way forward. I can see something different from all of this." In the video, Julibel nods in agreement. She leans into Alan's body. He holds her tightly. She says, "Yes, that's true." She smiles enormously—even though her face is wet from tears, which are still flowing, sliding over the dimples in her cheeks. Some viewers claim that they can see the collar of a bulky polo shirt poking out from her stained dress, if only for a moment, and still others claim that they can spot the painful outline of some great impossible geometry hov-ering around her person, just before she goes on, still nodding, and smiling, and crying, to assure us that "simply by doing the things that people already do everyday, or at least that which they could easily begin to do, we can collectively change the world. At breakfast. At work. At home. The inconceivable is within reach and is closer than we ever could have imagined."

TRYING TO HAVE SEX WITHOUT THINK-ING OF SEX

/ Lexi Cary

We taste like beer and coffee and bitterness
We wash each other like husks of rice
Powder never settling
Until you get bored of washing
And just eat it dirty
Because how dirty is rice anyway
It's not like licking the floor of a bar
Or kissing my exes
It is a clean dirt
The kind GOOP tells you to eat
I could never get over the image
Of Shailene Woodley eating dirt
And sunning her vagina
I have no private outdoor space
So I guess you'll just have to take me
dirty clean and unsunned
This pussy doesn't photosynthesize in the city

I mention Shailene Woodley like I'm trying to tell you
about some particular pressure of being a white woman
A pretty porcelain doll stuffed with patriarchy
Like that baby someone tried to take on a plane
that was actually just a husk of skin
Filled with coke I have nightmares about sometimes
And the flight attendant was like
Um, sir, why isn't that baby moving
And the answer was capitalism
But I'm a queer woman, so I'm not porcelain pretty,
but actually a Barbie with its hair shorn off,
stripped naked and buried in the yard,
gagging on soil, and there she goes about dirt again
Maybe her fucking uterus is writing this poem

Fertile earth   Fecund
                          Decadent
Stop   writing   about   your   ovaries   like   it's   something   new
                      We all have cramps

READING ANAÏS NIN IN A CAGE

/ Lexi Cary

There   aren't   enough   ways
To be   bound,   to be   held
Before   my   e x e c u t i o n

I'm both   on   the   platform
And   watching   from   below:
Dirty
        little
                     voyeur
Rubbing   rope   on   wrists—
    Noose
          perfume.

Is   it   weird
   When   my   past selves
watch   us   fuck?

   Kneeling,

      infinity mirrored,

  Coven circled,

      silent.

   G o o d w h o r e s .

Please   let   me   worship
Your   past   lives,
     Thank   them
For   bringing   You   to me,

Lick

        their

                feet,

Let

        them

            beat

               me,

If that's what they like.

I just want to be   agreeable,
Cast the right   spells,
To be kept   right here
For as long   as You'll have me,
Even if it's   forever,

Especially then.

F*CK THE WUNDERKINDER

/ Lexi Cary

At 26   I feel   I am running   out of time
to   "make it"   as a writer
at an age   where they'll still   want me
to pose   for Playboy,   because everyone knows
you can't   compose   a sentence   without
perky   tits   and   a   high,   tight   ass.

At 26   I lament   the time   I've spent
becoming a woman   who can   open   her mouth
without   a man's words   coming out,
wishing   I had been   puppeteered into early success,
only   to be   viciously   torn apart
by the   horny,   angry   pack of dogs.
We were supposed   to be   Dianas,   not Actaeons.

At 26   I am a walking   catalogue
of   young   success.
I know how   old   everyone   was
when they   got their   first   something.
And   this   numerology   of
BRITNEY,   BRITTNAY,   CHRISTINA,   CHRISTINA
ARIANA   and   AMY   and   ANGELINA
Does   no   magic   under   my   tongue.

At 26   I pore   over tweets   about   who made it
at   what   age.   I burn candles to Oprah.
I   reach   out
with   moisturized   hands,
drowning   in serum   and eye cream.
I   pray   for   baby   skin
so   that   someone   can   hand   me   what   I   want
and   c o r r o b o r a t e   their   narrative
of   exploiting   the   young.
It's   probably   a   sex   thing.

At 26   I know everything is a sex thing.
Especially   this feeling   of   f a i l u r e
implanted   invisibly   in   my   heart.
It   burns   like   warming   lube.
(Virginity   is   a   construct   because
we've   all   been   fucked   by   capitalism
before   even   taking   our   first   breath.
Go ahead   —   tell me otherwise.)

At 26   I pray   for the   wunderkinder
and the   one   hit   wonders,
the   child   stars
and   aging   bombshells.
I   pray   for   their   bonfire
to   set   sparks   to   what   made them.

I
     pray
          for
               everything
                         to
                              burn.

WE NEED HEAT STOKE THE FIRE v2.0.3 SteamRip (REPACK) xX(dEaDnAmE)Xx 78 SEEDERS

/ Døgtail Nørth

"If we could see ourselves as others see us, we would vanish on the spot." —Emil Cioran

set scene

the far end of the grocery store parking lot
Ø is in xir car

we hear as DEADNAME's big white truck pulls up
we hear the men and women and the not-so-muches and the we-
don't-exists and the everything-at-onces crying from the back of
his vehicle

we hear them before the motor

he yells out to xir
DEADNAME: what's up kike

xe looks blank in response to this
blinks and then speaks

Ø: haha not much dude what's good

DEADNAME and Ø bump fists

Ø speaks, an aside to the audience

Ø: i want my fist my fist i want him to feel the cold screaming
wind in it push through his collapse collapse bones obl i terate
ugly hick inbred fuck

    DEADNAME: sorry i was so late Dude you know how it is i had

to stop on the way here you know Man like my truck was making
a funny sound i think it was just the screams from the back though
maybe i'm not used to the sobs also had to help my buddy get his
quad away from the canals it like broke down you know how it is

Man

Ø, again speaking an aside to the audience, screaming, tearing at
xir hair

Ø: reach out and strangle that fuck

Ø, turns back to DEADNAME and speaks, visibly wincing at the
prospect of being around him
Ø: yeeaaaaah dude i know how it is, i got the 60 do you got it?

> **DEADNAME:** yeah i was only able to get you like 20 worth i
> made a few sales on the way here, you cool with just a dub?

Ø, aside to the audience, SCREAMING

Ø: slam his head in the fucking car door!

Ø, back to DEADNAME, looking a little pissed off but reluctant
to say anything

Ø: yeah dude that's cool no problem here you go

Ø hands a wad of cash to DEADNAME, DEADNAME gives Ø a
small baggie of RØT

> **DEADNAME:** if you wanna hang out later me and the boys are
> gonna have some fun you know what i mean

> a stronger wail emits from the back of DEADNAME's car

Ø, aside, again, subdued, mostly to xirself

Ø: kill him and then kill yourself

Ø, back to DEADNAME, clearly antsy and ready to leave

Ø: i'm busy the rest of today but i'll hit you up some time i'm not

DEADNAME: aight Dude, peace

DEADNAME drives off, Ø sits in xir car which starts floating upwards slowly, lights suddenly turn off

end scene

BITTERSWEET BIOGRAPHY 18 FROWNING DOGS—A NOTE ON BODIES AND MAGIC

/ Dogtail North

"isn't this silly and aren't you beautiful" — *Tsunami,* Told Slant

the scene is set. Static and notWind are standing acros —s from each other, a metal table between them. they are both scrubbed up, wearing surgical gloves, goggles, masks, and have a number of surgical implements at hand. in between and in front of them a white dog is pinned to a dissection tray, split open, its rib cage and lungs heaving at the open air, all in front of the blue curtain

notWind prods into the dog at its lungs with a long metal probe, emanating a small squeak from the dog and then speaks, mourn-fully

notWind: i wish i didn't exist

Static replies, a hint of desperation in its voice

Static: don't say that

notWind: this is horseshit, there's a reason i exist

it is getting a bit of harsh tone to its voice too now

Static: there's a reason i exist too, i don't like it either but you don't hear me complaining

zie replies, a little self-righteously

notWind: don't take that attitude with me, this is not the time, i'm serious

Static: i know, but how long have we been at this? you're com-plaining now?

zie is starting to run out of steam. at this point zie sounds more petulant than anything

                                              notWind: it isn't right

its voice softens

                        Static: you mean the reason we exist isn't right?

                        notWind: i don't know... all of this?

                        Static: we're necessary you know

                        notWind: i know...

                        Static: just as much as we're——

(in unison)

                        Static: inevitable

notWind: inevitable, look, i know; it just isn't pleasant, can you please be nicer about it? i'm a little on edge.

                        Static: i know, i'm sorry, i guess i'm really on edge too

                        notWind: that's no excuse

Static: you're right, i'm sorry for snapping at you, you did kind of take a tone with me there too

                        notWind: i'm sorry

                        Static: it's ok, it's getting late

throughout this entire conversation they are stitching small intricate sigils on the inside of the dog, they are filling it with rosemary, cloves, anise, rose petals and lemon peels

they pull down their surgical masks and kiss
                they are corporeal in this scene
                        they are completely androgynous
                            they are beautiful

with their surgical masks back in place, both of them return their
attention to the dog that is stuffed and splayed out in front of them

                Static: there's something special about this one

notWind speaks but with a pause, then softly

                        notWind: there shouldn't have to be

                            Static: i know.

They are both speaking softly now, their voices sullen, they exude
grief

        Static: i know… that's how it is though, out of necessity is how
                            we find them

zie speaks sternly

                    notWind: let's not dance around the topic

they both speak in harmony mockingly as if they'd said these words
their entire lives

                        notWind: it's them, it's their bodies

                            Static: it's them, it's their bodies

notWind is leaning over the dog, forcing a suction tube down its
throat. the clear surgical tubing leading away from it fills up with a
black tar-like substance

at the same time, still harmonizing—up until the last word

notWind: you step over the boundary you end up a fag

Static: when you step over the boundary you end up a dog

notWind removes the suction tube from the dog's throat and looks
up at Static

notWind: this duty is exhausting

Static, now looking at the dog's lungs its viscera still heaving up-
wards as if to escape
Static is acting coyly as if notWind is momentarily not in the room,
Statics' face is overcome with a thousand yard stare

Static: we are their patrons though, we have to

notWind is now looking down at the dog too. zie is obviously less
disassociated than Static

notWind: i know, i just wish they didn't need to… well… need
us

Static: i wish our job wasn't initiated by pain

notWind: me too… me too…

Static: they need our protection, our magic, the big ones can't
always win

notWind: they certainly can't with us around… well, eventually

Static: i mean, we can try

notWind leans down, pulling down hir mask, softly letting out
some incomprehensible but beautiful melody. Static harmonizes
notWind breathes gently and warmly into the open, floral filled
cavity of the dog. there is a quick, stong wind starting to pick up,
whipping both of them around, the blue curtain backdrop ripples
they both lay hands on the dissection tray and rotate it, to better

access the dog's face
notWind gently leans down to kiss the dog's face, Static pulls down
its mask and takes a turn
notWind shifts and kisses the dog's viscera, Static takes a turn
notWind shifts down further and kisses the dog's genitals
Static takes a turn

Both of their faces come up bloody. their faces are a strong mix-
ture of emotions. they make eye contact with each other briefly

notWind leans down gently and whispers into one of the dogs'
ears

notWind: i love you. it'll be ok. some day. maybe not now, maybe
      not later. maybe next birth. it'll come. i love you. it'll be ok.
          there's only so many worlds until home again.

notWind stands back up straight, almost glowing with a motherly
aura, Static is looking at hir in awe

      Static: you're never hotter than after a blessing

Static approaches notWind, circling around the table, and throws
its arms around hir, kissing notWind intensely as zie throws hir
arms around Static's neck and kisses it back.
Static pushes hir back onto an empty part of the table and gets on
top of hir. they are grabbing at each other, heaving like the viscera
of the dog

their movement knocks the tray from the table, the pins that held
the dog's body in place pop free, its wounds close up hastily—sig-
ils, stuffing and all—of their own accord
the dog jumps to its feet, immediately at attention, then briefly
sniffs around. it hears the commotion above it and scurries off
behind the blue curtain, still rippling with wind

Static and notWind melt into static

end scene

/ Dogtail North

I feel dizzy—I feel sick
I feel dizzy—I feel sick
I feel dizzy—I feel sick

this is what she whispered deep into my ear
bent towards me—bent inside me

i felt the fever in her fig trees, vibrating up through her parts and
into mine through the hip bone she hung on her childhood bed-
room wall
turning me inside out with our faces shared between us and it
stabbed me in the back of the throat (where the pain is located)
and i could feel it finally, in the fires being lit in the meat district
south of my vertebrae

we sneezed water out of ourselves and into each other and back
into ourselves until we had no more water to sneeze and waited
there, bruised as meat, for it to make sense again

and afterwards, in the quiet of our smolder, i asked the air and the
air asked me

can we stop?

CONTRIBUTORS' NOTES

Colleen Baran is a Canadian artist, designer, and writer. Baran's artwork has exhibited, and been published, internationally. Her poems have recently appeared in *Berkeley Poetry Review*, *Poetry Is Dead*, *The Impressment Gang*, and *Room Magazine*.

Paulette Beete's poems, short stories, and personal essays have appeared in journals such as *Crab Orchard Review*, *Provincetown Arts*, *Beltway Poetry Quarterly*, and *Pittsburgh Poetry Review*, among many others. She is also the author of the chapbooks *Blues for a Pretty Girl* and *Voice Lessons*. Her work has previously been nominated for the Pushcart Prize, and she has been a Winter Writing Fellow at the Fine Arts Work Center in Provincetown. She also blogs (occasionally) at thehomebeete.com, and you can find her on Twitter as @mouthflowers.

Dave Brennan's most recent book is *If Beauty Has to Hide* (Spuyten Duyvil). His poems appear or are forthcoming in *Conduit*, *Hotel Amerika*, *Obra/Artifact*, *Okay Donkey*, and elsewhere. He lives in Virginia and teaches at James Madison University.

Lexi Cary is a bi writer (w/b)itch and musician based in Los Angeles. Her work can be found or is forthcoming in *Germinal Mag*, *DUM DUM Zine*, and *Westwind*. She believes all poems are spells, all songs are poems, and worries that she'll never fully understand her birth chart. You can see more of her work at lexicary.com and @_lexicary on Twitter and Instagram.

Shane Jesse Christmass is the author of the novels *Belfie Hell* (Inside the Castle, 2018), *Yeezus in Furs* (Dostoyevsky Wannabe, 2018), *Napalm Recipe: Volume One* (Dostoyevsky Wannabe, 2017), *Police Force as a Corrupt Breeze* (Dostoyevsky Wannabe, 2016) and *Acid Shottas* (The Ledatape Organisation, 2014).

Brennan Emmett Cox currently lives and works in Baltimore, Maryland. He investigates abandonment and absence, creating portraits of human presence even where life appears to be absent. This past year, he was accepted into the Headstart Artist Residency in Barcelona where he taught several screen-printing workshops as well as displayed work in Barcelona's gallery district. He is a recent graduate from the University of Maryland, College Park, where he studied both English literature and painting. He has held exhibitions and residencies on the East Coast, in Barcelona, and in Lisbon.

Reilly D. Cox is an MFA candidate at the University of Alabama in Tuscaloosa where they serve as design editor for *Black Warrior Review*. They attended Washington College and the Bucknell Seminar for Younger Poets. They have work available or forthcoming by the Academy of American Poets, *Adirondack Review*, *Cosmonauts Avenue*, *Rust + Moth*, and others.

Rebecca Cross works as an editor in Vermont. Her poems have appeared or are forthcoming in *The Woven Tale Press*, *Breath and Shadow*, and *Monstering*.

Tony Mancus is the author of a handful of chapbooks, including *City Country* (Seattle Review), *Subject Position* (The Magnificent Field), *Bye Sea* (Tree Light Books), and *Apologies* (Reality Beach). He lives with his wife Shannon and three yappy cats in Colorado and serves as chapbook editor for Barrelhouse.

Dolan Morgan is a writer and illustrator living in Greenpoint, Brooklyn. He is the author of two story collections: *That's When the Knives Come Down* (A|P, 2014) and *Insignificana* (CCM, 2016). His work can be found in *The Believer*, at *Electric Literature's Recommended Reading*, on NPR, in a comic series on *The Rumpus*, and in the trash. Look for him online at dolanmorgan.com and on Twitter, @dolanmorgan.

Dogtail North is a transfemme witch and an ignorant multimedia artist and tattooist based out of the Pacific Northwest. She likes goblins and long walks on the beach and can be found on twitter at @horsetrauma.

Grace O'Connor grew alongside pine trees in the Catskills, New York. Currently, she is a rhetoric, composition, & teaching of English PhD student at the University of Arizona. She has work with *Rogue Agent Journal* and *The Adirondack Review*.

Cameron Pierce was the founding editor of Lazy Fascist Press. His most recent book is the nonfiction anthology *Taut Lines: Extraordinary True Fishing Stories* (Little, Brown UK). In 2015, he was the Mellon Writer in Residence at Rhodes University in Grahamstown, South Africa. He lives in Astoria, Oregon, with his wife and daughter.

Jen Rouse is the director of the Center for Teaching and Learning at Cornell College in Mount Vernon, IA. She is a two-time finalist for the Charlotte Mew Prize with Headmistress Press, and her most recent collection is entitled *CAKE*. Her chapbook *Riding with Anne Sexton* has just been reissued from Headmistress Press, and she has a chapbook forthcoming from Anti-Heroin Chic.

Gregg Williard's fiction, non-fiction, and visual art have been published most recently in *Fiction International*, *34th Parallel*, *Adelaide Literary Magazine*, *Raleigh Review*, and *X—R-A-Y Literary Magazine*. He teaches ESL to refugees and does a spoken word radio show, "Fiction Jones," on WORT community radio, wortfm.org.

www.ingramcontent.com/pod-product-compliance
Lightning Source LLC
Chambersburg PA
CBHW071926130726

47909CB00014B/2594